Swindon Photographers & Postcard Publishers

DARRYL MOODY

(Local Studies)

& PAUL A. WILLIAMS

LOC03

2019

First published in the United Kingdom in 2019

© Local Studies (Swindon Libraries & Information Service) 2019

Published for Local Studies (Swindon Libraries & Information Service)
Central Library, Regent Circus, Swindon SN1 1QG
www.swindon.gov.uk/localstudies

by The Hobnob Press, 8 Lock Warehouse, Severn Road, Gloucester GL1 2GA

Darryl Moody and Paul A. Williams have asserted their right under the Copyright, Designs and Patents Act 1988 to be identified as authors of this work.

LOC03

British Library Cataloguing in Publication Data
A catalogue record for this book is available from the British Library

ISBN 978-1-906978-67-9

Typeset in Adobe Caslon Pro. Typesetting and origination by John Chandler

Also available

LOC01   *Swindon's War Record* by W.D. Bavin (1922) 2018 facsimile reprint.

LOC02   *Roll of Honour 1939-1945: Swindon & District* by Katherine Cole

Cover images:
Front: W. Hooper in his Cromwell St. studio c. 1910.
Back: 1864 advertisement for R.K. Passmore.

CONTENTS

ACKNOWLEDGEMENTS

With grateful thanks to Andy Binks, John Chandler, Katherine Cole, Graham Light of Abbey Studios, Geoff Parker, Martin Norgate, Jon Ratcliffe, Josie Williams and many others for their help, insight, or the use of images from their private collections.

INTRODUCTION

There is an undeniable power in early photographs. They provide a window to our past with a vivid immediacy that is hard to match – documenting change and capturing history. For this reason, museums, archives and local studies libraries across the country continue to build extensive photographic collections, preserving this important visual record for future generations.

This publication was initially developed from a working document built up over many years by the Local Studies team at Swindon Central Library, gradually creating a list of local photographers, postcard publishers and others connected with the photographic history of Swindon and the surrounding area.

Then several years ago, Swindon's Local Studies Librarian Darryl Moody and local historian Paul A Williams discovered a shared interest in early Swindon photographers. They decided to pool their resources and see if they could create the definitive reference guide.

However, the authors have also drawn on existing resources. Most notably: a useful 1980s leaflet by Swindon Museums: *Checklist of Swindon Photographers: 1860-1960*; the highly-recommended 1985 monograph *Photographers in Wiltshire* by Martin Norgate (with Judith Blades and Pamela Slocombe); and Peter Sheldon's *Swindon in Camera*, which contains an excellent illustrated chapter on 'Swindon's photographic pioneers' (pp.54-75).

We have included all known individual professional photographers, partnerships, firms, postcard publishers (including some Post Office branches and stationers), and a number of more notable amateurs. We have also included a number of those who gave their occupation on the census as photographer, some employed 'inside' Swindon Works by the Great Western Railway. Generally we have not included the various national publishers who produced local postcards.

It is worth noting the variety of unusual and colourful names we have found working in this trade: Absalom, Hercules, Keylock, Lumkin, Shilk, Sigismund, Snook, and Zephaniah all make an appearance.

Many of these businesses mix and merge with each other, with a string of firms often occupying the same premises across decades. Furthermore, although the card mount for an Edwardian or Victorian cabinet card or *Carte de Visite* may provide enough details to date an image, a photographer may have continued to use existing stocks of these cards, even after their address or the business name had changed.

We hope that our book may prove useful in several ways:

- to help local photographs to be more accurately dated.
- to provide background historical information about local photography firms.
- to provide a biographical overview of the photographers themselves.
- to provide basis for further research into this profession and its social history

This project is necessarily a rather open-ended endeavour: more information will continue to come to light and information given here reflects the accuracy of those sources. Corrections, clarifications and additions are expected and always most welcome.

LOCAL STUDIES

Following a century of library provision by the GWR Mechanics' Institution, Swindon's first official Public Library opened on August 14th 1943, inside McIlroy's department store on Regent Street. By 1949 it had relocated to premises at Regent Street and the Reference Library opened inside the former Town Hall building. However, it was not until 1962 that the local history room opened, marking the official beginning of the town's Local Studies collection.

Local Studies hold a comprehensive collection of printed and published material relating to life in and around the Borough of Swindon: books, CDs, DVDs, maps, magazines, microfilm, newspapers, plans, slides, - and postcards and photographs. The Local Studies collection is located on Floor 2 of Swindon Central Library, and the experienced specialist team are on hand to help with any local history or family history enquiry.

PAUL A. WILLIAMS

Paul Williams, a retired financial administrator for W.H. Smith & the Research Council, has always had an interest in the history of Hinton Parva (or Little Hinton) where he was born and bred. Paul has published many books - his most recent, 'Farming Fields to Muddy Trenches' (2014), which was co-authored with Karin Thompson, commemorates those from Hinton Parva and Bishopstone who served and died in the Great War.

Paul is a notable postcard collector, with a focus on images captured by Swindon's most famous photographer William Hooper (1864-1955). Paul is related to William *via* William's 1890 marriage to Mary Jane Stroud of Aldbourne (Paul's paternal ancestor). Paul is always keen to hear from anyone who has photographs by Hooper or had contact with the family. Paul is also related to the 'Hammerman Poet' Alfred Williams (1877-1930) of South Marston: Alfred's sister Laura Charlotte Williams married Thomas Pill (Paul's maternal ancestor).

KEY TO REFERENCES, SOURCES & ABBREVIATIONS

All resources listed here are available in the Local Studies collection at Swindon Central Library. See the bibliography for further details:

Astill's: Astill's Almanac.
Bennett's: 1890 Reading business directory that covers the Swindon area.
ChambCom: The Swindon Chamber of Commerce directory.
CDV: *Carte De Visite* – a popular early photographic format.
COSP: Reference in 'Checklist of Swindon photographers'.
Dore's: Dore's Swindon Almanac and Public Register (1864).
Fletcher's: Fletcher's Directory of Wiltshire (various years).
GWR: The Great Western Railway.
Kelly's: Kelly's Directory of Wiltshire (various years).
Loyal: A Loyal Almanac (published in 1868).
NW Dir: North Wilts Directory (various years).
Pho Wilts: Reference in *Photographers in Wiltshire* by Martin Norgate.
PO Dir: Post Office Directory (various years).
SA&D: The 1869 Swindon Almanac & Directory.
S&D YB: Swindon & District Directory and Year Book (various years).
Swindon Dir: Swindon Directory, or Directory of Swindon (various titles).
Voters: Information extracted from voter lists (the electoral register).
WAM: Wiltshire Archaeological & Natural History Magazine.
W&SHC: The Wiltshire & Swindon History Centre (Chippenham).

SWINDON PHOTOGRAPHERS & POSTCARD PUBLISHERS

ABBEY STUDIOS LTD.

This business can claim to be the oldest ongoing photography firm in the region, as it is a continuation of a sequence of earlier firms dating back to that of Cirencester photographer Dennis Moss.

1977:	Abbey Studios Ltd. is started by Graham Light in October 1977. He purchased the Cirencester photographic business of Dennis Moss, with a history dating back to the late 1800s.
1982:	Abbey opens a commercial studio in Wood Street, Swindon.
1986:	Abbey takes over the business of Brian Cavill (formerly Cavill & Davidson) of Milton Road, Swindon. Later the Swindon businesses are closed and everything is operated from Cirencester.
1992 ChambCom:	Listed at 5 Whitworth Road, Swindon.

AINSWORTH, Walter see HART, William

ALLMAN, Charles Arthur (c.1871-1905)

According to the 1901 census, 'art photographer' Charles Arthur Allman was born in Paris *circa* 1871. He worked in Swindon and Bournemouth.

1901 Census:	In 1901 Charles is living at 221 Cricklade Road, Gorse Hill (his occupation listed as 'art photographer'), residing with his French wife Sophia and their son Henry.
1905:	Charles dies in Bournemouth on the June 27th 1905. His probate is then read in London on October 18th 1905, with effects of £191 6s left to his widow Sophia, and to Louis Stone (a fellow photographer). At this time he was living at 252a Holdenhurst Road in Bournemouth.

References:
Bournemouth Guardian: April 16th 1904, p.6 (advertisement).
COSP: 1901

LOST AND FOUND.

LOST, Monday, May 6th, tiny brown smooth DOG, answers to Pup; finder rewarded.— ALLMAN, Photographer, Gorse Hill.

C. A. ALLMAN & CO.,

The well-known ARTISTS & PHOTOGRAPHERS of the Bois de Boulogne Studio,

252a, HOLDENHURST ROAD, BOURNEMOUTH,

For the most Charmingly Finished Crayon and Water Colour Enlargements. Also High-class and Up-to-date Photographs can be had at the above address. Prices Moderate. Inspection Invited.

Pho Wilts: 221 Cricklade Road, Swindon (1901).
Swindon Advertiser: May 17th 1901, p.4 (notice for Charles' lost dog 'Pup').

ARTIS, R.J.

In August 1854, notices appeared in the Wilts & Gloucestershire Standard advertising the services of Mr R.J. Artis – the 'celebrated London photographer' who had set up temporary premises at 6 Bath Buildings, Old Swindon. This very early photographer was working before any Swindon studio was in operation. This may be the Robert J. Artis found on the 1871 census living at Alma Road in Hemel Hempstead, with his occupation given as 'photographic artist'.

Swindon.

Mr. R. J. Artis has been taking Photographic likenesses in this town, and as a proof of the accuracy, we noticed a little child three years of age recognize three portraits in succession; this is a strong proof of their faithfulness. Those who wish to have their likenesses taken, should give Mr. Artis an early call, as his stay in Swindon is but short. We refer the reader to his advertisement in another column for his address.

PHOTOGRAPHY.

MR. R. J. ARTIS, the celebrated London Photographer, is now paying a short visit to Swindon, and has opened rooms to take portraits on collodion at No 6, Bath Buildings, Old Town.

R. J. A. has already met with a large amount of patronage, from the Nobility and Gentry, and his rooms are now daily crowded; his portraits being far superior to any others yet produced!!

Price from 3s. 6d. to 15s. 6d., complete, in frame and morocco case.

*Notices from the Wilts and Gloucestershire Standard, August 5th 1854, p.1

AULT, Frederick Horatio Walker (1846–1914)

Frederick H.W. Ault was an 'artist and general photographer' from Dudley.

1846:	Frederick is born January 4th 1846 at Netherton, Dudley in Worcestershire.
1854:	Christened aged 8 at Darlaston on October 26th 1854.
1881 Census:	School House, Otterhampton, Bridgwater ('photographer/

science teacher').

1891 Census: Living at Ogbourne Village, Ogbourne St Andrew, Marlborough ('photographer/artist').

1901 Census: 246 Ferndale Road, Manila Terrace, Swindon ('photographer/artist')

1911 Census: Living in Stanford-in-the Vale, Berks. Frederick and Sophia are both listed as photographers.

1914:   Frederick dies June 27th 1914, aged 69. He is buried at St. Deny's, Stanford-in-the-Vale, Berkshire, on June 29th 1914.

References:

Devizes & Wilts Gazette: April 3rd 1884, p.2 (article on the Duke of Albany).

Devizes & Wilts Gazette: June 14th 1888, p.3 (court case).

www.oxfordtimes.co.uk/news/3742643.Lifting_the_Vale/

http://viewfinder.english-heritage.org.uk/story/intro.aspx?storyUid=20

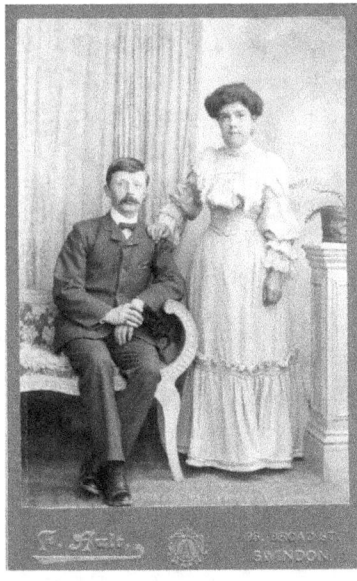

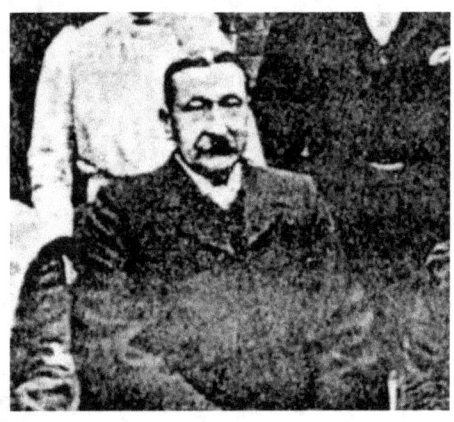

Frederick Horatio Walker Ault (1845–1914).

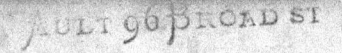

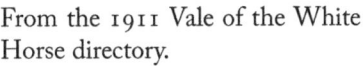

From the 1911 Vale of the White Horse directory.

FARINGDON.

F. H. W. AULT,

ARTIST & GENERAL PHOTOGRAPHER,

STANFORD-IN-THE-VALE. BERKS.

Also at FARINGDON Tuesdays during the forthcoming Season.

High-class Photographs and Photo Picture Postcards of neighbourhood and chief places of interest.

Orders for Private Views, Groups, &c., will receive prompt attention on receipt of postcard or letter.

Prices moderate compatible with good work. High-class references submitted

BAKER, Charles Henry (1866–1943)

1866:	Born at Rubery in Bromsgrove.
c1887:	Marries Georgina Deakin in Kings Norton.
1901 Census:	21 Lorne Street ('railway messenger' in GWR Swindon Works).
1903 Kelly's:	Listed as 'photographer' at 21 Lorne Street, Swindon.
1911 Census:	21 Cambria Place (recorded as 'messenger' at GWR Swindon Works).
1943:	Charles dies in Swindon.

References:

COSP:	1903
Pho Wilts:	21 Lorne Street, Swindon (1903).

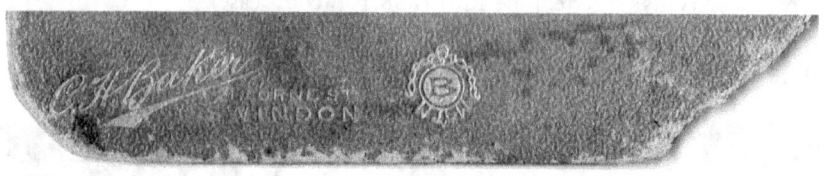

BANBURY, Arthur Edward (1878–1935)

Arthur Banbury was a Devon-born photographer with several premises in Swindon.

1878:	Arthur Banbury is born in Exeter.
1881 Census:	36 Portland Street, St. Sidwell, Exeter.
1891 Census:	Parr Street, Exeter ('scholar').
1901 Census:	Cardrew House, Redruth (Boarder, 'photographer').
1903 NW Dir:	Premises listed at 25 Faringdon Street & 23 Fleet Street, Swindon.
1904:	He marries Caroline (Carrie) Louisa Harris at St. Mark's Church.
1907 NW Dir:	Premises listed at 25 Faringdon Street & 23 Fleet Street, Swindon.
1911 Kelly's:	Listed as 'photographer, 25 Faringdon Street'.
1911 Census:	25 Faringdon Street, Swindon. His wife Carrie is recorded as 'assisting in the business'.
1912:	Arthur joins the Freemasons at Gooch Lodge, Swindon.
1915 Kelly's:	Premises listed at 88 Cricklade Road, 25 Faringdon Street, and 23 Fleet Street.
1916:	He joins the Royal Engineers (Inland Water Transport) at Swindon on November 27th 1916. Employment declared as 'photographer'.

1920 Kelly's:	Listed as 'photographer, 23 Fleet Street & 25 Faringdon Street'.
1920 NW Dir:	Listed as 'photographer, 25, Faringdon Street, and 23 Fleet Street'.
1935:	Arthur dies aged 56 in Exeter.

References:

COSP:	1905-1922.
Pho Wilts:	25 Faringdon Street, Swindon (1907-1919).
Pho Wilts:	88 Cricklade Road, Swindon (1915).
Pho Wilts:	Fleet Street, Swindon (1915).
Pho Wilts:	25 Faringdon Road, Swindon (1920).
Pho Wilts:	23 Fleet Street, Swindon (1909-1920).

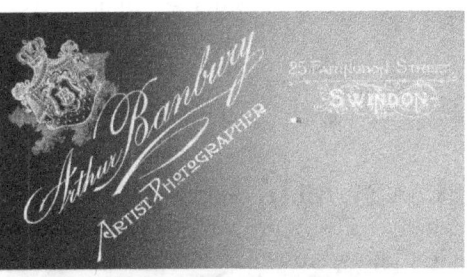

BARKER, George

George Barker was one of a number of photographers employed by the GWR.

1891 Census:	Working as a 'railway labourer'.
1901 Census:	75 Commercial Road, Swindon ('photographer').
1911 Census:	Living at 3 Fairview, Swindon ('photographer').

BATHE, Horace Richard Ulundi (1892-1954)

The GWR staff records list a Horace Bathe - initially as a 'shop clerk' and then as an 'asst. photographer and printer'. We note with interest that Ulundi is regarded as the final battle of the Anglo-Zulu war and it occurred on July 4th 1879 (July 4th is Horace's birthday). We presume this was the inspiration for his unusual middle name, given that family members served in Africa at that time.

1892:	Horace is born in Swindon on July 4th 1892.
1911 Census:	Living at 32 Dixon Street, Swindon with his parents ('photographer').
1917:	Marries Marian Louise Hughes in Bedwellty, Monmouth-shire.
1939 Register:	Living at 11 Oxford Street, Swindon (occupation given as 'photographer – railway studio staff. Aerial photography R.A.F. photostat operator').
1954:	Horace dies December 3rd 1954 in Swindon, aged 62.

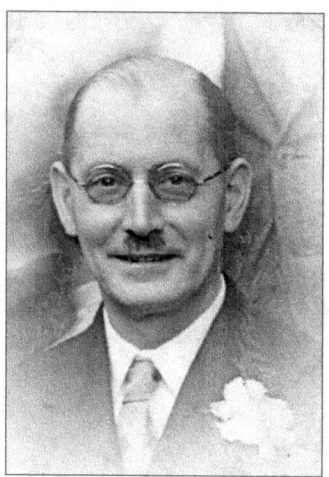

BEANEY, Albert George (1913–2006)

Albert Beaney was a well-known amateur photographer, best known for his street photography depicting local children from the 1940s onwards. He had worked in the GWR Swindon Works, then left to join the RAF during the Second World War. After being demobbed Albert worked in the Post Office until his retirement in 1973. The road 'Beaney View' in Moredon was named after him.

A collection of around 40,000 Beaney images are held at Swindon Museum & Art Gallery (a combination of 7000 prints and 33,000 individual negatives). This collection was acquired with assistance from the Swindon Society. In 2011 an exhibition of his work ('Back to Black and White') was held in Theatre Square, in conjunction with his family and the Swindon Society. Swindon heritage magazine ran a series of features on his work from their very first issue onwards.

1913:	Born in Swindon on October 22nd 1913.
1939 Register:	Living at 50 Beatrice Street, Swindon. His occupation is given as 'unemployed French polisher working as photographer own account'
1946:	Marries Joan Newmarch in Scunthorpe.
1951 S&D YB:	50 Beatrice Street, Swindon.
1952 S&D YB:	Listed under 'photographers' at 50 Beatrice Street, Swindon.
2006:	Albert Beaney dies in Swindon aged 93.

References:

Child, Mark: *The Swindon Book* (entry on pp.31-32).
Swindon Advertiser: July 2nd 2011, p.11 ('Back to Black and White' exhibition).
Swindon Advertiser: April 19th 2012, p.3 (article on the naming of Beaney View).
Swindon Heritage: Summer 2013 (no.2), pp.16-17.
Swindon Heritage: Autumn 2013 (no.3), pp.48-50 ('Beaney and the Bogies').
Swindon Heritage: Winter 2013 (no.4), pp.28-29 ('Back to Beaney').
Swindon Heritage: Spring 2014 (no.5), pp.73-75.
Swindon Heritage: Summer 2014 (no.6), pp.74-75.
Swindon Heritage: Winter 2014 (no.8), pp.42-43.

THE BEAUMONT STUDIO see BEAUMONT, Henry Archibald

BEAUMONT, Henry Archibald

H.A. Beaumont was a postcard publisher operating in Gorse Hill, Swindon. The back of an early *carte de visite* shows the printed name of H.A. Beaumont, Tewkesbury with an added hand written note *'Late of* Tewkesbury, *King William St, Swindon'*:

1871:	Henry is born in Gloucestershire *circa* 1871.
1893:	He marries Ellen Hopkins in Tewkesbury.
1901 Census:	Oldbury Road, Tewkesbury ('town postman').
1907 Kelly's:	88 Cricklade Road, Swindon.
1910 Voters:	88 Cricklade Road, Swindon.

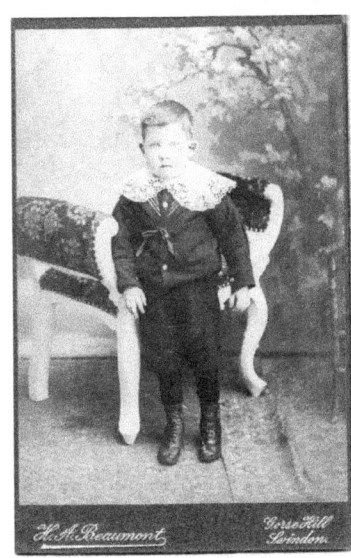
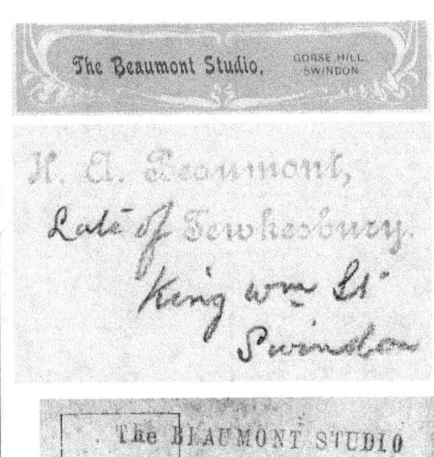

References:
COSP: 1906-1910
Pho Wilts: 88 Cricklade Road, Swindon (1909).

BEARD, Donald

Donald Beard was a 1960s Swindon photographer based at 29a Commercial Road and at Regent Circus.

1967 Fletcher's: Listed as 'photographers & photographic dealers, Regent Circus, Swindon'.

BETTS, Alfred Alexander (1858–1928)

From 1879 to 1882 Alexander Betts was one of the managers of the Soho Bazaar School of Photography. Soon after his 1887 marriage he relocated to Swindon, setting up his photography business in Old Swindon, after which they moved to Flyde in Lancashire. Betts' address is sometimes given as 'Prospect Villas'. His business was taken over by two short lived photographic businesses, **John William HUFF (Wilson Huff)** and then **Henry DOBBINSON**.

1858:   Born in 1858 at Brighton.
1887:   Marries Mary Isabell Davies on October 29th 1887 at St. Peter's Church in Blackburn (source: FamilySearch website).
1889 Kelly's: Prospect Place, Old Swindon.
1891 Census: Living at Prospect Place in Swindon ('photographer').
1895 Kelly's: 59 Prospect Place, Old Swindon.
1901 Census: 49 Livingstone Terrace, Fleetwood, Fylde ('photographer').
1911 Census: 49 Blakiston Street, East Fleetwood, Lancashire ('photographer').
1928:   Alexander dies in 1928 aged 70.

References:
Child, Mark: *The Swindon Book Companion*, pp.20-21.
COSP: 1889-1898.
Pho Wilts: Prospect Place, Swindon (1890).
Pho Wilts: Prospect Place or Lane, Swindon (1893-1895).

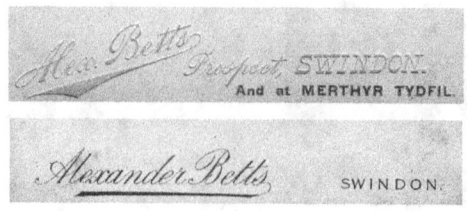

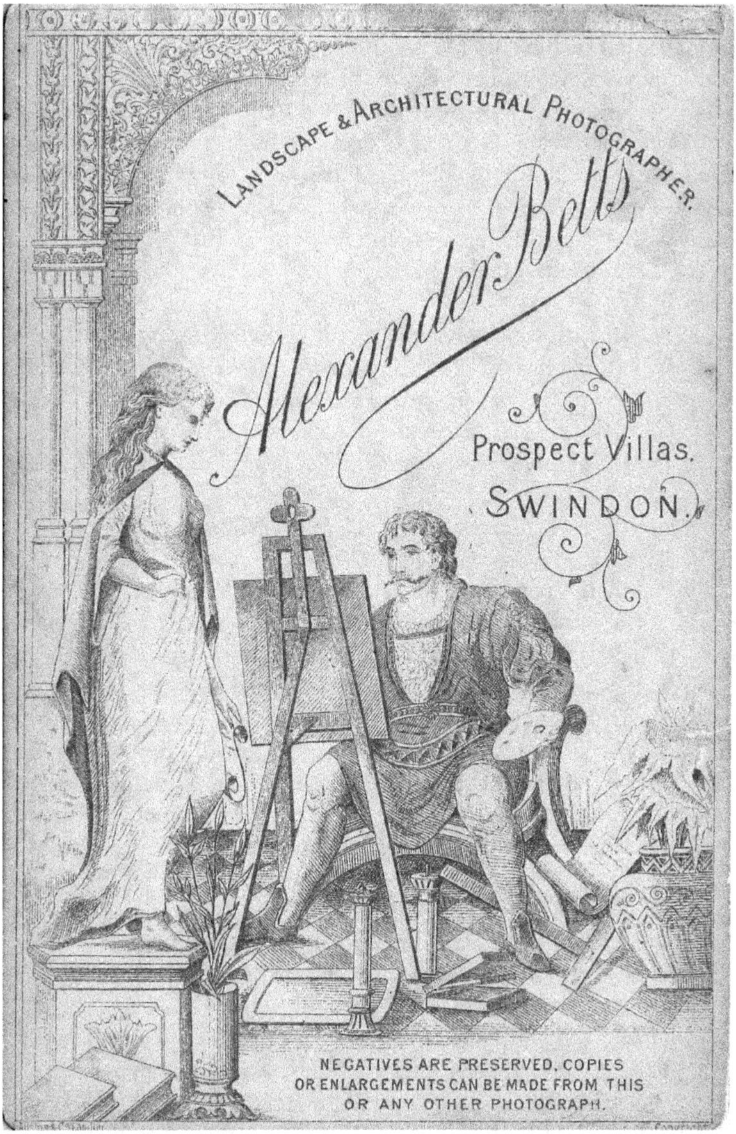

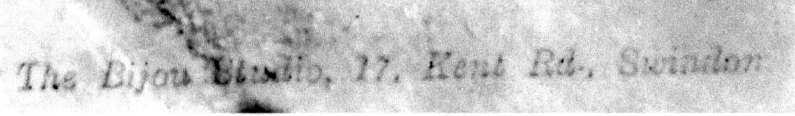

THE BIJOU STUDIO

Located at 17 Kent Road, Swindon, this studio is found on some 1906 postcards of the funeral procession for the Swindon tram crash victims.

The Bijou Studio, 17, Kent Rd., Swindon

BIRD, Denis Herbert R. (1923–2001)

Denis Bird was a notable photographer, historian, artist, founder member of the Swindon Society, and a warden of Holy Rood Church. He was born on June 19th 1923 in Maesteg in Glamorgan, Wales. His father was from Shropshire and his mother was from Swindon. They met when his father was stationed at Chiseldon Camp during the Great War. As a child the family lived in Penygraig in the Rhonda Valley. The family then moved on to Bridgend, which is where Denis first became interested in photography:

While I was still at grammar school in Bridgend, I developed an interest in photography. My first camera as a boy was a Box Brownie. This hobby has been of great interest to me all my life and I have thousands of photographs and slides. I find photographing buildings the most absorbing. I have taken hundreds of photographs of Old Town. A lot of them have been published in various editions of Swindon in Retrospect.
From an interview with Denis Bird in *Millennium Memories*.

It was his father's premature death from tuberculous which prompted his mother to move back to her hometown of Swindon around 1940. Denis began to work 'inside' the GWR Swindon Works as a junior clerk. During the Second World War he served in the Royal Engineers in Egypt and Malta. In 1975 Denis published his book *The Story of Holy Rood: Old Parish Church of Swindon*. Dennis died October 6th 2001. After his death, his collection of negatives and contact sheets was donated by Pam Bridgeman, *via* the Swindon Society, to the Wiltshire & Swindon History Centre (with the assistance of Chairman Andy Binks). Swindon's Local Studies collection includes many examples of his work.

References:
Child, Mark: *The Swindon Book* (entry on pp.36-37).
Old Town Group: *Millennium Memories* (interview with Denis Bird, pp.19-22).
Old Town Mag: November 2001 (obituary for Denis Bird, pp.14-15).
Swindon Advertiser: October 18th 2001 ('The man who brought town's history and photography to life has died').
Swindon Advertiser: October 22nd 2001 ('Denis Bird: The man who loved Swindon').

BLEASDALE, Richard Henry (1838–1897)

A Victorian commercial photographer who in the 1880s published a volume of early photography inside the GWR Swindon Works (see bibliography). He took circa 3000 photographs during his life, beginning c1857. He visited the works of many of the main railway companies, of course, including the GWR.

1838:	Born in Chipping, Lancashire.
1871:	Marries Mary Ann Creboo on August 6th 1871 at Bunbury, Cheshire.
1861 Census:	22 Deepdale Terrace, Preston, Lancashire ('spindle maker').
1871 Census:	Olive Street, Liverpool ('photographer & artist').
1881 Census:	136 Park Road, Aston, Warwickshire ('photographer & publisher').
1897:	Richard dies aged 59 in Worcestershire.

References:

Bleasdale, R.H.:	Album of photographic views of the Great Western Railway Locomotive & Carriage Works, Swindon (London, published by the author, circa 1881).
Gray, A. (ed.):	'Richard Henry Bleasdale 1837–1897', in The Spooner Album, Seymour Memorial Edition (Garndolbenmaen: RCL Publications, 2003)

BOLLARD, Beatrice

Beatrice Bollard Studios Ltd. was a prolific portrait, wedding and commercial photographer established in 1959. Her work included commissions for Arkell's Brewery. An advertisement for Beatrice Bollard appears at the back of Peter Sheldon's 1979 book *Swindon in Camera*.

1961 Phone Book:	38(?) Victoria Road, Swindon.
1965 Fletcher's:	31 Victoria Road, Swindon.
1967 Fletcher's:	31 Victoria Road, Swindon.
1967 Swindon Dir:	31 Victoria Road, Swindon.
1970 Swindon Dir:	31 Victoria Road, Swindon.
1973 Swindon Dir:	31 Victoria Road, Swindon.
1979:	35 Havelock Street, Swindon.

1979 advertisement.

SWINDON IN CAMERA – CONTINUES
WITH PHOTOGRAPHIC SERVICES
FOR ITS PEOPLE, COMMERCE
AND INDUSTRY BY –

Beatrice Bollard
STUDIOS LTD

SWINDON'S PORTRAIT, WEDDING AND
COMMERCIAL PHOTOGRAPHERS
(ESTABLISHED 1959)

PHOTOGRAPHIC SERVICES
AND

	ART DEPARTMENT
Wedding	
Portrait	Frames
Commercial	Albums
Passport and Identity	Artists' Original Paintings
Old Photographs Copied and Restored	Reproduction Prints
	Framed Pictures
Developing and Printing	Craftware and
Mounting	Ancillary Lines of Unique Design
Heat Sealing	

35 HAVELOCK STREET, SWINDON
TELEPHONE 35176

BOWERING, Ernest Arthur (1891-1973)

1891:	Ernest is born February 26th 1891 in Swindon.
1911 Census:	Living with his parents at 70 Hythe Road, Swindon ('photographer').
1920:	Ernest is listed in the Great Western Railway staff records as a printer. Records show that he first worked 'inside' from 1920, then was laid off in 1921 ('reducing hands'), before returning in 1923.
1939 Register:	Living with his wife Dorothy M. Bowering at 82 Argyle Street, Gorse Hill, Swindon. His occupation is given as 'blue printer & mounter Railway Drawing Office Staff'.
1973:	Ernest dies in Swindon aged 82.

BRAMWELL-HILL, William Charles see HILL, William Charles Bramwell

BROOKS, Henry James (1838-1925)

Artist and photographer Henry Brooks operated in both Abingdon and Old Swindon. His Swindon premises were located at 5 Bath Terrace on Bath Road, sometimes given as 'Literary Institute, Bath Terrace, Swindon'.

1838:	Born in Birmingham.
1865:	Henry's business taken over by **Edward BUTLER**.
1871 Census:	The Vineyard, St. Helen, Abingdon ('portrait artist & photographer')
1881 Census:	The Poplars, Abingdon St. Helen, Abingdon ('portrait painter photographer'). His daughter Emily is recorded as 'portrait assistant'.
1925:	Henry dies in Essex aged 86.

References:

Child, Mark:	*The Swindon Book Companion* (entry pp.23-24).
COSP:	1863-1865
North Wilts Herald:	September 9th 1865 (Notice regarding **Edward BUTLER**).
Pho Wilts:	Bath Terrace, Swindon (1864-1865).
Swindon Advertiser:	October 10th 1864, p.1 (advertisement).
Swindon Advertiser:	August 28th 1865.
Swindon Advertiser, October 10th 1864.	

Literary Institute, Bath Terrace, Swindon
CARTE DE VISITES, of exquisite beauty
and Artistic arrangement, are being taken at
the above address by HENRY J. BROOKS, Artist
and Photographer.

CARTE DE VISITE
PORTRAITS:

Inferior to none for Excellence of Finish and Permanence, at a price considerably below
what is usually charged for First-Class productions, at

BROOKS'S

PHOTOGRAPHIC ESTABLISHMENT,

BATH TERRACE, SWINDON.

Terms, - 12 for 10s. 6d.

Horses, Dogs, Landscapes, and Architectural Views Photographed. Paintings, Engravings,
and Photographs Copied.

PHOTOGRAPHS FINISHED IN OIL AND WATER COLOURS.
☞ CHARGES EXTREMELY MODERATE.

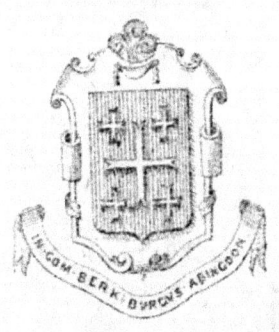

HENRY J. BROOKS.

Artist & Photographer

ABINGDON & SWINDON.

BRYANT, John

1935 Kelly's: 13 Regent Street, Swindon.

References:
Pho Wilts: 13 Regent Street, Swindon (1935).

BUCKLAND, Ernest Augustus (1863-1936)

1863:	Ernest is born February 6th 1863.
1877:	Begins work for the Great Western Railway on March 31st 1877. Staff records show he became an assistant photographer in the Drawing Office.
1911 Census:	Living with his wife Mary Lydia Buckland at 82 Cheltenham Street, Swindon ('photographer' for the Great Western Railway).
1936:	Ernest dies in Swindon.

BUTLER, Edward (c1810–1894)

In 1865 Edward Butler took over the business of **Henry J. BROOKS** at 5 Bath Terrace, Swindon. In 1866 he went into partnership with **George KING**, of Devizes Road, forming **Butler & King**. Edward left Swindon in 1869, returning to his family in Reading and continuing as an 'artist portrait photographer' until his death in 1894.

c1810:	Born in Benson in Oxfordshire.
1841 Census:	Butts, St Mary, Reading ('artist').
1851 Census:	St. Mary's Butts, Reading ('portrait painter').
1861 Census:	Living at 9 St. Mary's Butts, St. Mary, Reading ('photographic artist carver and guilder'). Sons Edward and John assisting in the business.
1865:	Takes over the Swindon business of **Henry J. BROOKS**.
1869:	Leaves Swindon and returns to Reading.
1871 Census:	St. Mary's Butts, Reading ('artist photographer').
1881 Census:	No.9 St. Mary's Butts, Reading ('portrait and landscape artist').
1891 Census:	St Mary's Butts, Reading ('artist portrait painter').
1894:	Edward dies March 1st 1894 aged 85, at no.9 St. Mary's Butts in Reading. He is buried at London Road Cemetery in Reading, on March 6th 1894.

References:

Child, Mark:	*The Swindon Book Companion* (entry pp.26-27).
COSP:	1865-1866
Pho Wilts:	Devizes Road (1866).
Reading Mercury:	March 3rd 1894, p.5 (death notice and short obituary).
Swindon Advertiser:	August 28th 1865 (notice regarding 5 Bath Terrace).
North Wilts Herald:	September 9th 1865.

The death of an old and respected townsman, Mr. Edward Butler, of St. Mary's Butts, will be heard by many with much regret. He passed away on Thursday evening, after a long and weary illness, in his 85th year. In artistic circles his sound and experienced advice, especially to amateurs in painting, will be greatly missed.

Reading Mercury, March 3rd 1894.

IMPORTANT NOTICE.

PHOTOGRAPHIC STUDIO,
5, BATH TERRACE, SWINDON.

HENRY J. BROOKS begs to inform the Gentry, Clergy, and Inhabitants of Swindon and Neighbourhood, that he has relinquished the business lately carried on by him at the above address in favor of Mr. E. Butler, who has had the charge of it for the last ten months. H. J. B. takes this opportunity of returning his sincere thanks for favors received, and to solicit a continuance of the same on behalf of his successor.

EDWARD BUTLER, in succeeding to the above business, hopes, by strict attention and prompt execution of all orders, to merit a continuance of those favors so liberally accorded to Mr. Henry Brooks.

E. B. having had twelve years practical experience in the profession, guarantees first class Photographs on reasonable terms. Landscape and Architectural Photography by special arrangement.
5, Bath Terrace, Swindon,
August 18th, 1865.
All persons having claims on Mr. Brooks for the Swindon Branch are requested to forward particulars to 5, Bath Terrace.

Swindon Advertiser, August 28th 1865.

BUTLER AND KING

This was the joining of the two photographic businesses of **Edward BUTLER** and **George KING** in 1866. They operated at Devizes Road (then also known as 'Short Hedge') until 1869 when Edward Butler left and returned to Reading. At this time George King went into partnership with **Zephaniah DODSON** until his death in 1872.

References:
COSP: 1865-1866
Pho Wilts: Devizes Road, Swindon (1866).

BUTLER, James Mellor (c1857 - ?)

James Mellor Butler seems to have previously been part of a partnership with George Taylor named 'A. & G. Taylor' at Baldwin Chambers, Baldwin Street, in

Bristol (see London Gazette, April 23rd and 30th 1897). James then continued the business alone – and set up premises in Swindon the following year.

c1857:	Born at Westminster, London.
1899 Kelly's:	Listed at 28 Regent Street, New Swindon.
1901 Census:	33 Duke Street, Brighton, Sussex ('manager, photographer').

References:

COSP:	1898-1899
London Gazette:	April 23rd 1897.
London Gazette:	April 30th 1897.
Pho Wilts:	28 Regent Street, Swindon (1898-1899).
Swindon Advertiser:	July 24th 1897, p.5 (notice of demolition).

> Cistern at their premises in Fleet-street. It was resolved
> that notice be served on Mr J. M. Butler, photographer,
> calling upon him to pull down the building erected by
> him at the rear of 28, Regent-street, without first
> having his plans approved by the Council. Mr James
> Hinton made application to abandon a 30ft street being

Swindon Advertiser, July 24th 1897.

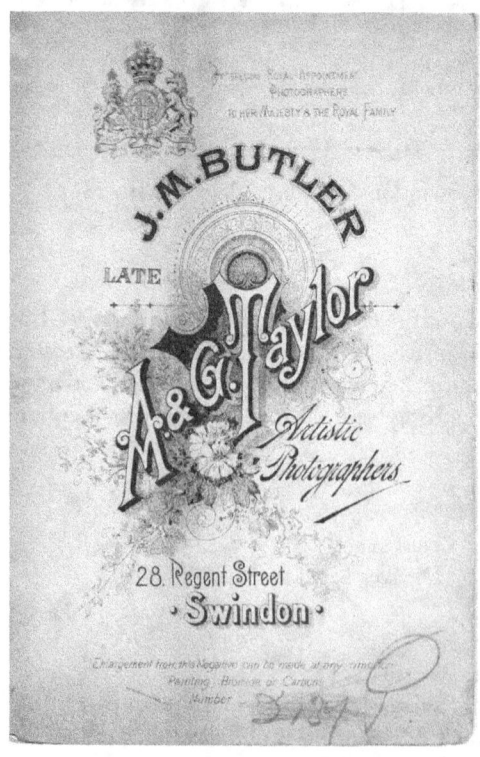

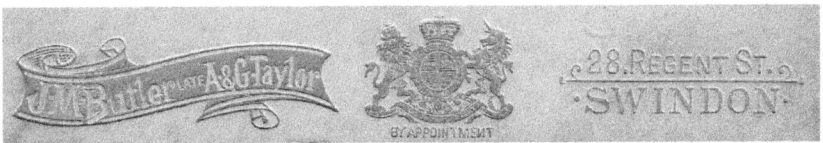

CALYX PHOTO SERVICES LTD.

Calyx in the long-running business of local photographer **Richard WINTLE**. They are a notable picture and TV agency with a specialist archive of images of the Royal Family and an archive of local news photographs stretching back of 30 years.

References:
Website: http://calyxpix.com

CANNON, Charles (1824–1885)

Charles Cannon may have been the earliest professional photographer of New Swindon. His premises at 30 Regent Street were later to be occupied by **James Smith PROTHEROE.**

PHOTOGRAPHY.

SPECIAL NOTICE FOR ONE MONTH ONLY.

C. CANNON,

PHOTOGRAPHER, NEW SWINDON,

HAVING purchased the " Negatives" recently held by the GREAT WESTERN PHOTO-GRAPHIC COMPANY, which also include Portraits, Views, &c., taken by the late MR SHORT, of Swindon, and Mr. CHURCH of Wotton Bassett and Calne, begs to inform his Friends and Customers that

PORTRAITS AND VIEWS OF THE NEIGH-BOURHOOD,

taken by himself and the above-named may be had at *half the usual price* on application at
30, REGENT STREET, NEW SWINDON.

TERMS—Cash with order. Not less than half dozen to be ordered at one time.

A large assortment of unmounted Photos for Scrap Books may be had at the following prices :—

Packets containing	1 doz.	...	2s. 6d.
,,	,,	2 doz.	...	4s. 6d.
,,	,,	3 doz.	...	8s. 0d.

Swindon Advertiser, July 26th 1880.

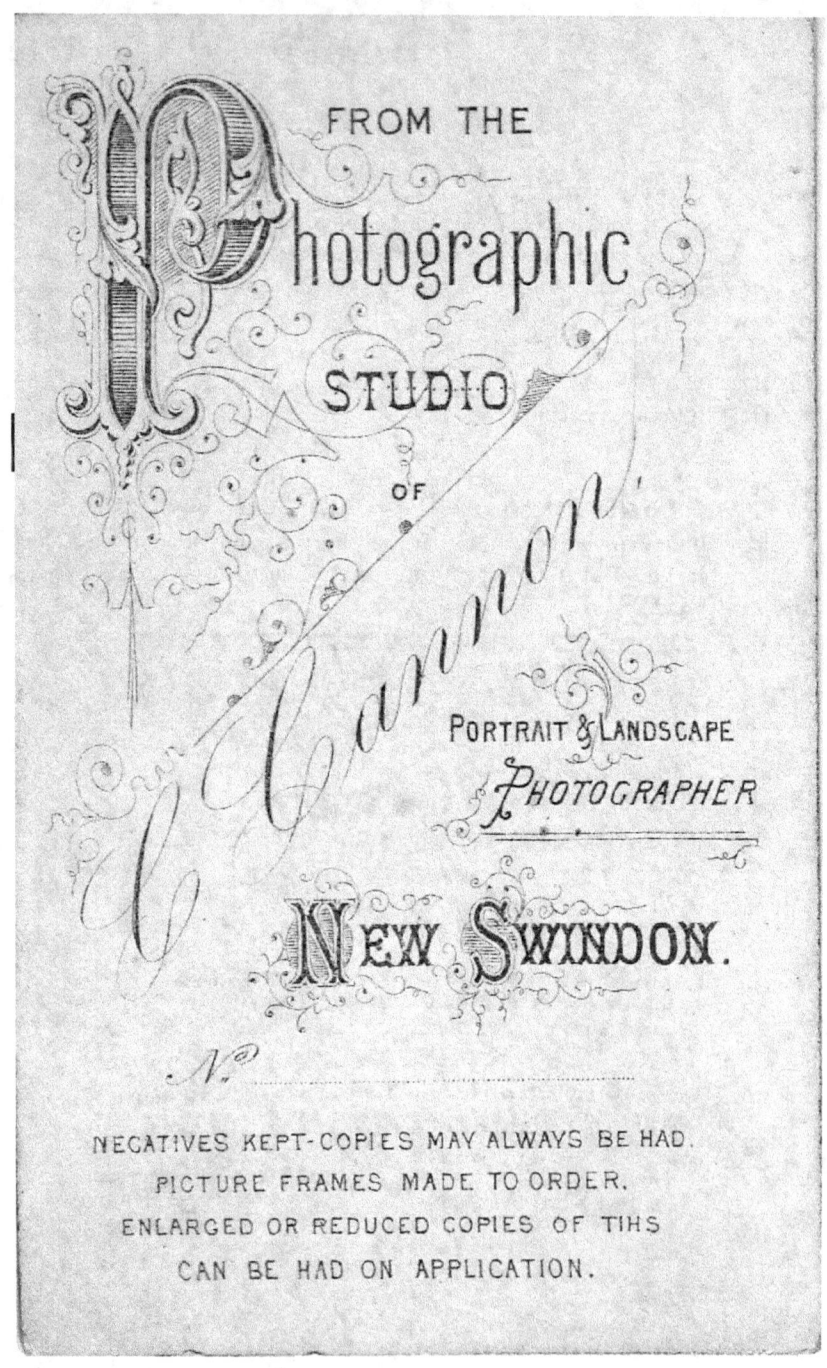

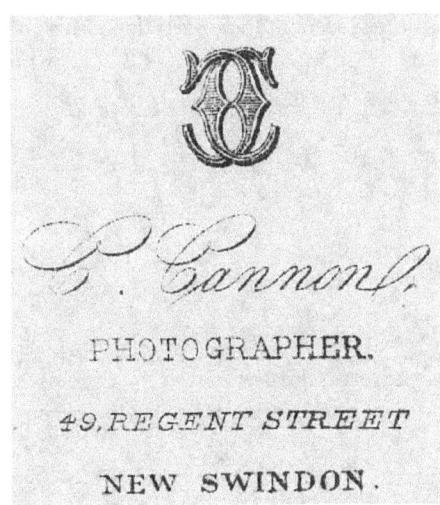 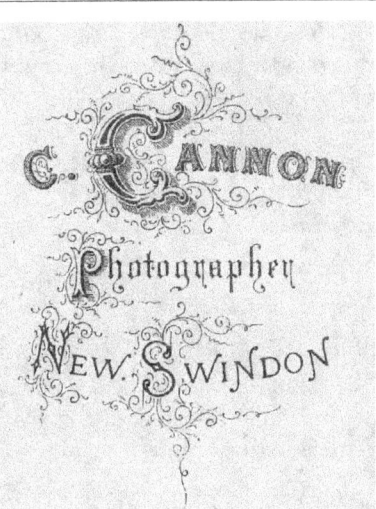

1824:	Charles is born in 1824 at Chilton in Berkshire.
1851 Census:	Newport Street, Old Swindon ('tailor & outfitter').
1871 Census:	49 Regent Street, New Swindon ('photographer').
1880 Kelly's:	30 Regent Street, Swindon.
1880:	An advertisement in the Swindon Advertiser declares that Charles Cannon has recently purchased the negatives of the **Great Western Photographic Company**, which included photographs taken by **William SHORT** and 'Mr Church of Wootton Bassett and Calne'.
1881 Census:	30 Regent Street, New Swindon ('photographic artist')
1885:	Charles dies September 16th 1885 at Chiseldon, aged 62.

References:

Child, Mark:	*The Swindon Book Companion* (entry p.28).
COSP:	1871-1884
Pho Wilts:	49 Regent Street, Swindon (1872-1875).
Pho Wilts:	Regent Street, Swindon (1878).
Pho Wilts:	30 Regent Street, Swindon (1880-1882).
Pho Wilts:	Chiseldon (1885).

Swindon Advertiser: July 26th 1880, p.3 (advertisement).
Swindon Advertiser: September 19th 1885, p.4 (death notice).
Swindon Advertiser, September 19th 1885.

CARR, E.

Little is known about E. Carr, who appears as a photographer in the 1915 North Wilts Directory at 15 Regent Street. There was a studio at this address which produced the only known local examples of so-called "stickyback" photographs. These unusual, small-format portraits with a gummed back were a cheaper and less formal product. Stickyback portraits often seem more relaxed than others of that period. However, we have not been able to establish if it was E. Carr who offered this service.

1915 NW Dir: 15 Regent Street.

References:
COSP: 1915.

THE CENTRAL BAZAAR

The Central Bazaar published postcards from around 1912, from their premises at 41 Bridge Street, Swindon (with a copyright notice from Protheroe and Simons on the front).

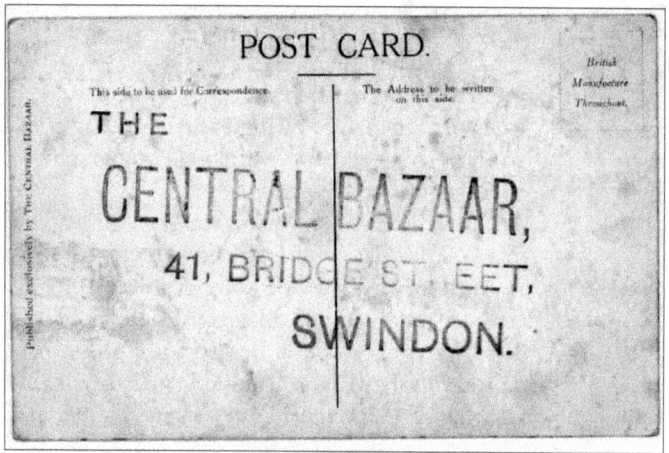

CHANDLER, F.

A Chiseldon 'Stationer & Confectioner' based at 3 Turnball

Pub. by F. Chandler, Stationer & Confectioner,
        3 Turnball, Chisledon, Wilts.

CHARLES, H.

Little is known about this Victorian photographer, but an 1893 notice in the *Swindon Advertiser* seems indicate that it was a very short lived firm which went out of business and had its assets sold at auction by Messrs James Hinton & Son 'instructed by Mr Charles'.

TO AMATEUR PHOTOGRAPHERS & OTHERS,
**AUCTION MART, REGENT STREET,
NEW SWINDON.**

MESSRS. JAMES HINTON & SON are instructed by Mr CHARLES, to SELL by AUCTION, at the above, on FRIDAY, February 3rd, 1893, A PHOTOGRAPHIC STUDIO, 20ft. by 9ft. (10ft. glass and 10ft. Corrigated Iron), 2 Half-plate Cameras, Lenses, Burnishers, &c., &c., all in Good Condition.

The above may be viewed during the week previous to Sale at 18, Commercial Road, New Swindon.

Also a Quantity of HOUSEHOLD FURNITURE comprising Bedsteads, Beds Tables, Chairs, &c., &c.

Sale to commence at 7 o'clock.

References:
COSP: 1893
Pho Wilts: 18 Commercial Road, Swindon (1893).
Swindon Advertiser: January 28th 1893, p.1 (auction notice).

COCKELL, J.M.
J.M. Cockell operated in the 1940–1950's at 98 Broad Street, Swindon.

References:
COSP: 1950s

COLLIER, D.G.
References:
COSP: 1947

COLVILLE, Frank
1920 Kelly's: Listed as 'Colville,
                    Frank, photographer, 130 Victoria Road'.
1920 NW Dir: 130 Victoria Road.

References:
COSP: 1919-1921
Pho Wilts: 130 Victoria Road, Swindon (1920).

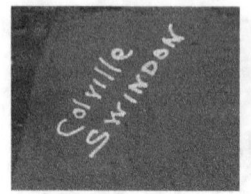 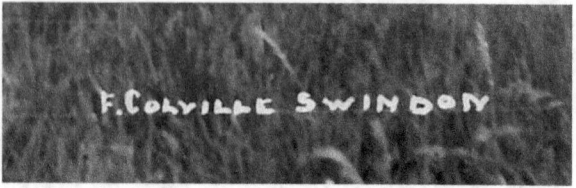

COWIE, Ethel May [*née* Absalom] (1884–1950?)

1884:	Born in Swindon on February 19th 1884.
1901 Census:	70 William Street, Swindon ('photographer's assistant).
1911 Census:	70 William Street, Swindon, with her daughter Ettie Cowie. No occupation is given.
1939 Register:	Living at 138 Princes Street, Swindon ('interviewer Littlewoods Mail Order Stores').
1949/50:	Ethel dies in Swindon aged 65.

References:
COSP: C1915–1920S

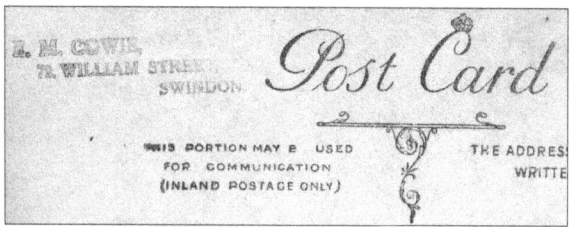

COX, George (1865–1916)

George Cox was an Edwardian 'sub-postmaster and newsagent' who published postcards in Gorse Hill, Swindon.

1865:	George is born in Hungerford, Berkshire.
1884:	Marries Emily Bungay.
1901 Census:	250 Cricklade Road, Gorse Hill, Swindon ('stationer & printer').
1903 Kelly's:	Listed at 250 Cricklade Road, Gorse Hill, Swindon ('newsagent, printer & post office').
1907 Kelly's:	90 Cricklade Road, Gorse Hill, Swindon.
1911 Census:	90 Cricklade Road, Gorse Hill ('sub postmaster,

newsagent').

1916:	George dies and is buried at Whitworth Road Cemetery, Swindon, on 23rd August 23rd 1916.
1920 Kelly's:	Business now listed as 'Cox, Emily (Mrs.), news agent, printers, & post office, 90 Cricklade Road, Gorse Hill'.
1939 Register:	Widow Emily Cox is recorded at 90 Cricklade Road in Gorse Hill.

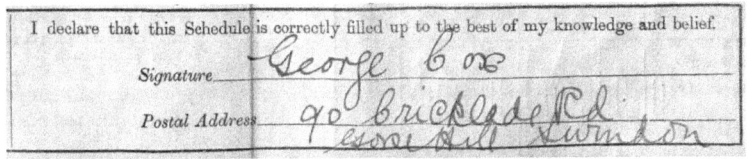

Signature of George Cox from the 1911 Census.

DEAVIN, Ernest A. (1880?–1940?)

Little is known about this local photographer. Details initially came from a single *carte de visite* circa 1905. Premises located at 27 North Street, Swindon.

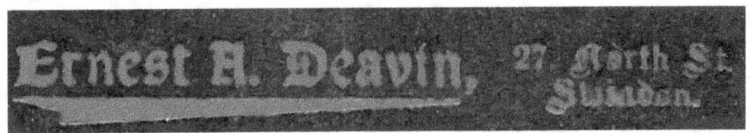

DECENT, John Wheaton (1874–1954)

John W. Decent once ran the Tower Stores in Wroughton. See also **Thomas KING**.

1874:	Born on January 29th 1874.
1891 Census:	Church Street, Brixham, Totnes, Devon ('ironmonger').
1901 Census:	North Terrace, St Ives, Penzance ('ironmonger').
1906:	Baptised on May 10th 1906 at Mere.
1904:	Marries Augusta Palmer in Mere.
1911 Census:	Living at Castle Street, Mere ('shop assistant').
1923 Kelly's:	Wroughton (Ironmonger).
1931 Kelly's:	Listed as 'ironmonger, Wroughton'.
1939 Register:	17 Grove M Milton, Weston Super Mare ('ironmonger – retired').
1954:	John dies aged 80.

References:

Wroughton LHG:	*Wroughton History*, Part 2, pp.117-118 (overview of Tower Stores).

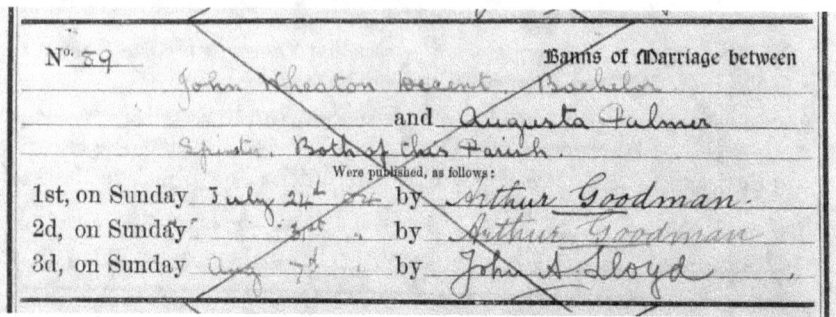

DOBBINSON, Henry (1872–1956)

1872:	Henry is born in Darlington, Durham.
1891 Census:	30 Gordon Street, Broughton, Salford, Lancashire ('photographer').
1901 Census:	22 Lethbridge Road, Swindon ('boarder, photographer').
1910:	Marries Alice Kate Bromwich.
1911 Census:	300 Kensington Liverpool, West Derby ('photographer').
1956:	Henry dies aged 84.

References:
COSP:	1901
Pho Wilts:	59 Prospect Lane, Swindon (1901).

DODSON, Zephaniah (1846–1931)

Zephaniah Dodson's family came to Swindon in 1869. In that year Zephaniah went into partnership with **George KING**, whose studio was located in Devizes Road. They traded as **Dodson & King**. George King died in 1872 and Zephaniah Dodson continued on his own, working as an 'artist photographer' at 58 Prospect Place. In 1883 moved his business to 58 Regent Street and over the next decade or so had premises at 19 and 28 Regent Street. He retired in 1895 and became an agent for parcel delivery companies at his home in 39 Eastcott Hill, Swindon.

1846:	Zephaniah is born in 1846.
1865:	Marries Sarah Albinia Lane.
1875:	Prospect, Swindon ('portrait and landscape photographer').
1880 Kelly's:	Prospect, Swindon ('photographer and tobacconist').
1881 Census:	Living at 58 Prospect, Old Swindon with his wife, six children and his mother-in-law ('artistic photographer')
1883 Astill's:	Announces a move from Prospect to new premises at 58 Regent Street, New Swindon.
1889 Kelly's:	19(?) Regent Street, New Swindon.

1890 Bennett's:	Listed at 20 Regent Street, New Swindon ('photographer').
1891 Census:	39 Western Street, Swindon (Enumerator may have made a mistake and he may still have been at Eastcott Hill).
1893:	A fire at Zephaniah's (uninsured) studio causes £10 of damage.
1901 Census:	Living at 39 Eastcott Hill, Swindon.

MR. Z. DODSON, of Prospect, Swindon, photographer, has sent us some specimens of a new style of photographic portrait which he is now introducing to public notice, and which he calls the cabinet portrait. The style is specially adapted for portraits of the carte-de-visite size, and is so arranged as to form an important adjunct to the portrait, making it appear as though fixed in a very handsome frame, with surrounding embellishments, some of which are of characteristic design. For instance, members of the Masonic body may have the surroundings emblematic of the craft, whilst those who affect the literary style (the common *possé* assumed by people when sitting for their portrait) may have the surroundings to consist of books negligently placed with writing material, inkstands, the midnight lamp, &c., &c. Altogether the style is very effective, and we think likely to become popular.

Swindon Advertiser, March 31st 1877.

with his tender.

A FIRE broke out on Friday evening at Mr Z. Dodson's photographic studio in Regent-street, New Swindon, and did considerable damage before it was extinguished. It appears that Mr Dodson left the premises about six o'clock leaving a lighted lamp hanging up in the shop. When he returned twenty minutes afterwards he found the studio in flames. With the assistance of Fireman Munday, who was fetched from the Public Offices, and several passers-by, the flames were extinguished, but not before damage to the extent of about £10 had been done. Fortunately the fire did not reach a quantity of fireworks which were stored in a box waiting for the 5th of November. It is stated that Mr Dodson has previously insured his premises annually for the past twenty years, but this year he neglected to renew.

Swindon Advertiser, October 28th 1893.

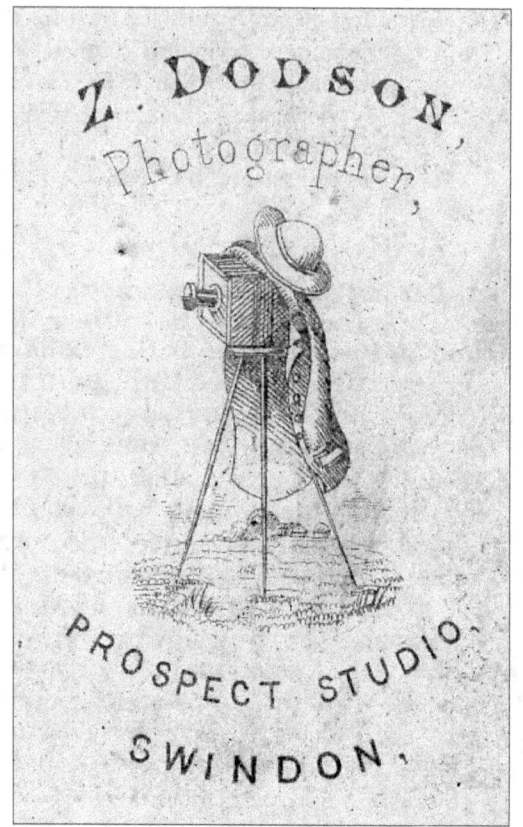

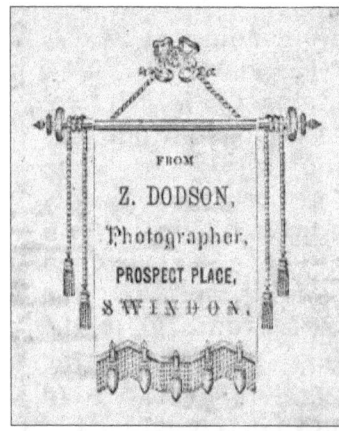

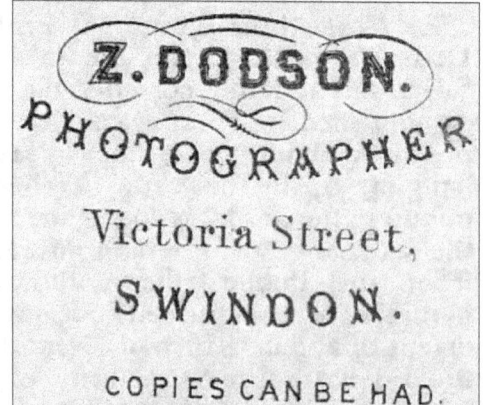

1903 Kelly's:	Listed at 89 Victoria Rd, Swindon: 'agent for Sutton & Co., parcel conveyance'.
1911 Census:	Living at 39 Eastcott Hill, Swindon.
1915 Voters:	Living at 170 Victoria Road.
1918 Voters:	Living at 170 Victoria Road.
1920 Kelly's:	Listed as 'Agent for Sutton & Co., Parcel Conveyance, 170 Victoria Road'.
1931:	Zephaniah dies in Swindon aged 85.

References:

Child, Mark:	*The Swindon Book Companion (*entry on pp.43-44).
COSP:	1871-1897
Pho Wilts:	Prospect, Swindon (1872-1880).
Pho Wilts:	46 Prospect Place, Swindon (1877).
Pho Wilts:	28 Prospect Road, Swindon (1882).
Pho Wilts:	58 Regent Street, New Swindon (1885-1887).
Pho Wilts:	19 Regent Street, Swindon (1890).
Pho Wilts:	Regent Street & Sanford Street, Swindon (1893).
Pho Wilts:	28 Regent Street, Swindon (1895).
Swindon Advertiser:	May 10th 1875, p.8 (advertisement).
Swindon Advertiser:	March 31st 1877, p.4 (announces new 'cabinet card' format).
Swindon Advertiser:	April 13th 1889, p.3 (court case v. James Lott).

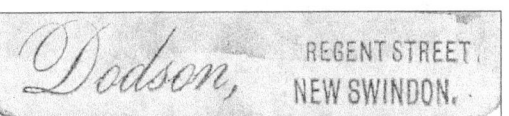

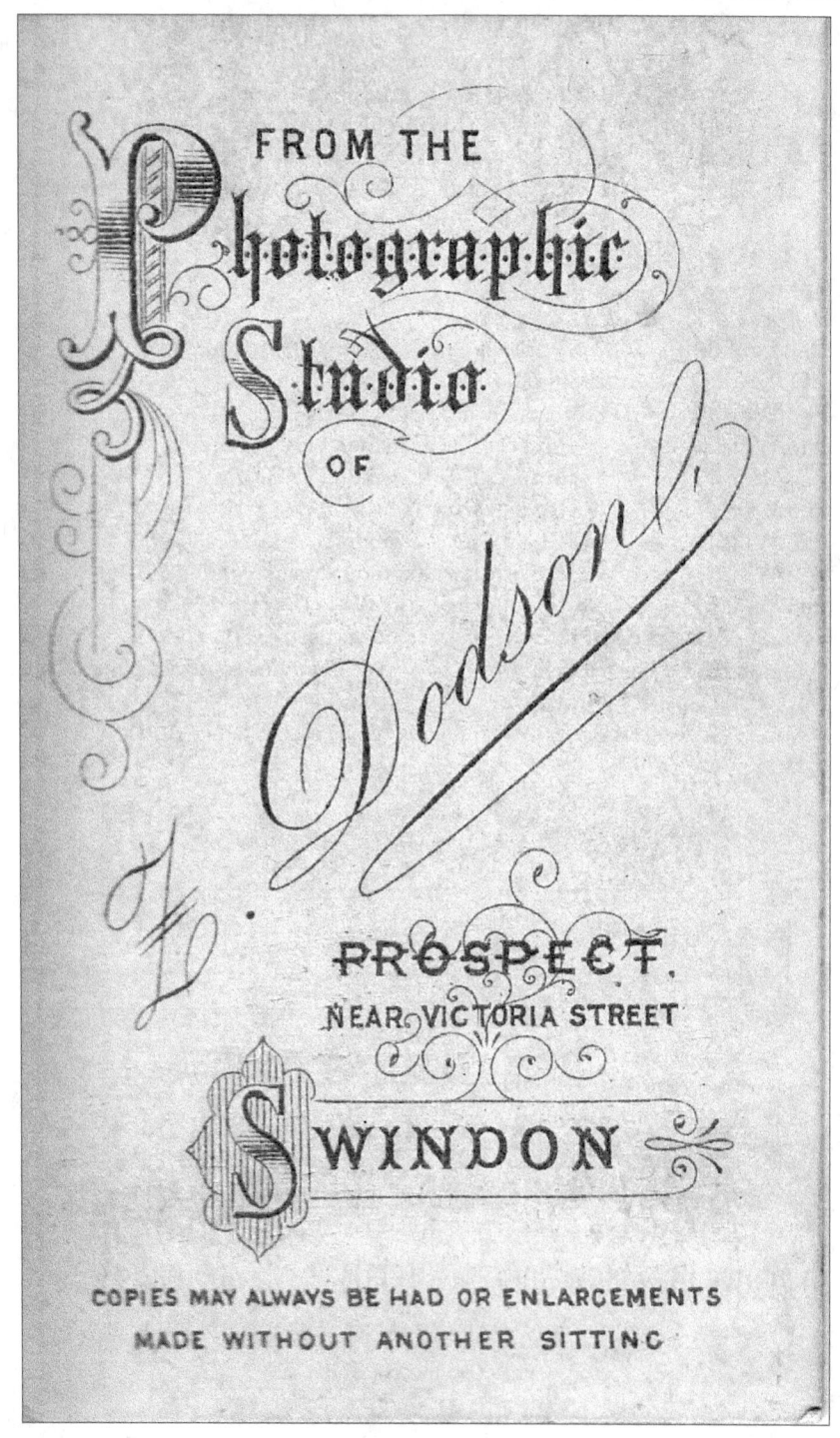

Swindon Advertiser: July 22nd 1893, p.8 (court case v. William Clarke).

Swindon Advertiser: October 28th 1893, p.4 (fire at his studio).

Swindon Advertiser: February 10th 1894, p.3 (Zephaniah in court as a witness to an incident where a cow in Regent Street smashed its head through the window of McIlroy's, directly opposite his studio).

Swindon Advertiser: May 18th 1895, p.4 (court case v. John Toomer & Sons).

Swindon Advertiser: August 14th 1894, p.6 (court case v. W. Greenaway & Son).

Richard Sheldon: *A Swindon Camera* (pp.58-61).

Wilts & Glouc Standard: April 20th 1872, p.5 (court case v. Albert New).

Wilts & Glouc Standard: May 11th 1872, p.5 (court case v. Albert New).

DREW, John

John Drew was a stationer and postcard printer with premises at 51 Bridge Street, Swindon. Some of his postcards are simply marked as 'Drew' and others also mention premises at 'Aldershot & Farnboro'. John Drew is also notable for printing the first edition of 'Swindon's War Record' by W.D. Bavin (1922), the comprehensive account of the town's role in the Great War, and the 'Swindon Strike Bulletin' (1920).

1920 Kelly's: Listed as 'Stationer, 51 Bridge Street'.

1920 NW Dir: Listed as 'Bookseller and stationer, agent for the North Wilts Herald' at 51 Bridge Street.

References:

Swindon Advertiser: December 20th 1907, p.3 (Thanking him for producing the programme for the 21st annual show of Swindon's 'Fur and Feather' Association).

Wiltshire Times: October 11th 1919 (a public apology to Chippenham's MP).

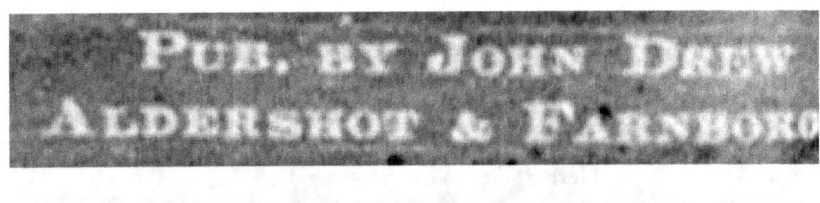

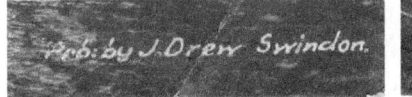

OFFICIAL NOTICES.

Re RAILWAY STRIKE.

WE, the undersigned, as the printers of the Swindon Strike Bulletin, dated and issued the 2nd October, 1919, hereby apologise to George Terrell, Esquire, M.P. for the Chippenham Division of Wiltshire, for the following untrue and defamatory statements reported to have been made by him at a meeting at Cricklade on the 1st October, 1919, and published by the Strike Committee at Swindon, namely:

1. That he advised the people to boycott the strikers and prevent them from obtaining rations.

2. That he deserved even more than being chased off the platform.

3. That he stated to one of our strikers if he would return to work he would secure for him a good job on the railway for the remainder of his career.

JOHN DREW (PRINTERS) LTD.,

Printers,

51, Bridge Street,

4265 Swindon.

On Saturday 11th October 1919, this public notice from John Drew appeared on the front page of the Wiltshire Times & Trowbridge Advertiser, apologising to George Terrell, the Conservative MP for Chippenham.

DURNFORD, Herbert Charles (1893–1919)

1893:	Herbert is born in Trowbridge, Wiltshire.
1911 Census:	Living at Redstocks, Melksham ('Ironmonger assistant').
1918:	Marries Lilian Tilling in Swindon.
1919:	Herbert dies in Swindon aged 26.

References:

COSP:	1918-1919
Pho Wilts:	130 Victoria Road, Swindon (1919).

EAGLE PHOTOGRAPHIC SERVICE

1952 S&D YB: Listed at 6 Cricklade Street.
1959 Fletchers: 6 Cricklade Road, Swindon.
1960 Swindon Dir: 6 Cricklade Street, Swindon.

EASTER, John Samuel (1837–1922)

John Samuel Easter was a very early Old Swindon photographer based at
'Short Hedge' - which is an early name for Devizes Road.. He had left the
photography profession by 1871 to become the landlord of the Engineers
Arms on Cheltenham Street, followed by another career as a 'cycle and motor
mechanical engineer'!

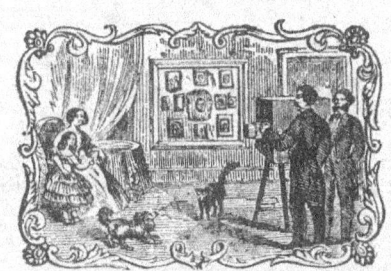

J. S. EASTER,
PHOTOGRAPHER,
SHORT HEDGE, SWINDON.

PHOTOGRAPHIC PORTRAITS in any style, on Paper, Leather,
Cloth, Iron, & Glass.   Also for Brooches, Lockets, Pins, Rings, &c.
Carte de Visite Portraits from 10s. 6d. per dozen ; Photographic
Portraits from 6d. Upwards.   Miniatures Copied.

c1837:	Born in Suffolk.
1864 Dore's:	Listed at Short Hedge, Old Swindon.
1865:	He marries Martha Watts.
1871 Census:	Living at 30 Union Street, Swindon ('fitter – GWR Works').
1881 Census:	Living at the Engineers' Arms public house, 49 Cheltenham Street, New Swindon ('beer house keeper').
1889 Voters:	49 Cheltenham Street, New Swindon.
1891 Census:	Landlord at the Engineers' Arms ('beer house keeper & blacksmith').
1901 Census:	28 Fleet Street, Swindon ('cycle mechanic').

| 1911 Census: | Living at 41 Cheltenham Street, Swindon ('cycle & motor mechanical engineer'). |
| 1922: | John dies aged 86 and is buried on September 10th 1922 at Radnor Street Cemetery in Swindon. |

References:

COSP:	1862–1865
Pho Wilts:	Short Hedge, Swindon (1864).
Pho Wilts:	Devizes Road, Swindon (1865).
Swindon Advertiser:	December 9th 1878, p.5 (court case).

EDWARDS, Ernest Frank (1889–1966)

1889:	Born on March 1st 1889.
1916:	Marries Lily B. Clifford in Swindon.
1918 Voters:	Ernst Frank Edwards and Lilian Bessie Edwards living at 69 Radnor Street, Swindon.
1920 NW Dir:	Living at 69 Radnor Street.
1939 S&D YB:	Living at 69 Radnor Street.
1939 Register:	69 Radnor Street, Swindon ('photographer & picture framer')
1966:	Ernest dies in Swindon aged 77.

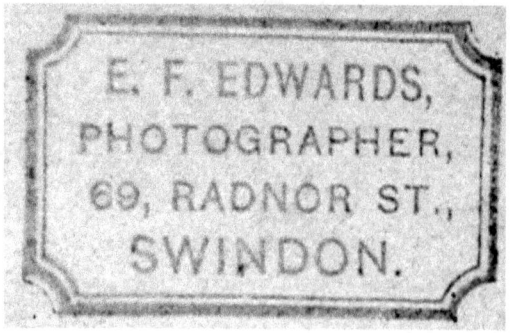

References:

| COSP: | c1923 |

EDWARDS, G.

Embossed imprint on postcard with 'G. Edwards, 280 Ferndale Road, Swindon'.

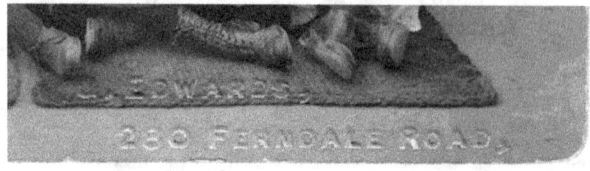

EMPIRE STUDIOS
1936 S&D YB: 13 Regent Street, Swindon.

References:
COSP: 1934-1937

> EMPIRE STUDIOS,
> 13, Regent Street, Swindon

FERNEL (or FERNEE), Mrs Ada (1852–1913)
Ada's surname is given as 'Fernée' in the 1907 Kelly's directory and on the 1911 census, but as 'Fernel' on the back of at least one postcard. Following her death in 1913, the business seems to have been continued at the same address by Miss Margaret Fernée.

1852:	Ada King is born in London circa 1852.
1880:	Marries Stanley Edward E. Fernee in London.
1907 Kelly's:	Fernée Ada (Mrs.), fancy stationer & servants' registry office, 76 Victoria Rd.
1911 Census:	Ada is living at 76 Victoria Road, Swindon ('Fancy shop lending library and servant registry'), with three daughters and one son (but no husband).
1913:	Ada dies on March 25th 1913, aged 61.
1920 Kelly's:	The business is now listed as 'Fernée, Margaret E. (Miss), fancy stationer, 76 Victoria Road'.
1920 NW Dir:	Listed as 'Fancy dealer, 76 Victoria Road'.

> Pub. by A. Fernel, Stationer & Fancy Goods Importer, 76 Victoria Road, Swindon.

From the reverse of a postcard (with 'Fernel' spelling)

> FERNEE Ada of 76 Victoria-road Swindon **Wiltshire** (wife of Stanley Edward Ericke Fernee) died 25 March 1913 Probate **London** 18 April to Marguerite Evelyn Fernee spinster. Effects £189 4s. 3d.

1913 Probate of Ada Fernee.

FEW, Robert (1828–1913)
Born in 1828, Robert Few lived to the age of 85, an unusually long life and something that was noted in his widely published obituaries. His game and poultry shop on Wood Street seems to have been a target for many shoplifters,

with numerous court cases in the local press for the theft of hares, rabbits, pigeons, and pig tongues! He seems to have been a well-known local character and in one letter to the Swindon Advertiser he signs himself as 'The Audacious Few'.

1828:	Born at Potterne near Devizes. Baptised 16th March 1828.
1844:	Entry in J.G. Harrod & Co. directory.
1856:	Marries Sarah of Marlborough (according to the 1911 census).
1868 Voters:	Living at Wood Street, Swindon.
1869 SA&D:	Listed as 'Provision dealer, Wood Street'.
1871 Census:	24 Wood Street, Old Swindon ('dealer in game').
1881 Census:	24 Wood Street, Swindon ('poulterer & gamekeeper').
1890 Bennet's:	24 Wood Street ('poulterer').
1901 Census:	24 Wood Street, Swindon ('poulterer & shopkeeper').
1911 Census:	139 Victoria Road, Swindon ('retired poulterer').
1913:	Robert dies in Swindon aged 85. The Gloucester Journal describes him as 'Swindon's oldest tradesman'.

References:
Cheltenham Chron.:	October 11th 1913, p.4 (lengthy obituary).
COSP:	1862-1868
Gloucester Journal:	October 11th 1913, p.12 (death notice).
Pho Wilts:	Wood Street, Swindon (1865).
Swindon Advertiser:	December 14th 1874 p.4 (theft of rabbits from his shop).
Swindon Advertiser:	September 20th 1884, p.5 (ongoing controversy over the destruction of some plums from Mr Few's shop).
Swindon Advertiser:	October 18th 1884 (letter: 'Mr Few and his plums').
Swindon Advertiser:	December 25th 1903, p.5 (account of an accident caused by runaway horse, from which Robert Few had a narrow escape).
Swindon Advertiser:	May 26th 1905, p.11 (Robert is prosecuted by the R.S.P.C.A. for animal cruelty towards his horse).
Swindon Advertiser:	December 22nd 1905, p.7 (wedding anniversary).

A GOLDEN WEDDING.- Mr and Mrs Robert Few, of Wood Street, Swindon, celebrated their golden wedding on Wednesday in the last week, the 13th inst., when over thirty members of the family, including children and grandchildren, assembled and honoured the event. It is gratifying to note that the aged couple are in fairly good health, and were the recipients of many presents.
Swindon Advertiser, December 22nd 1905, p.7.

SWINDON'S OLDEST TRADESMAN
DEATH OF MR R. FEW

Swindon's oldest tradesman, Mr Robert Few, died on Tuesday at the age of 85 years. The son of a farmer of Potterne, near Devizes, Mr Few went to Swindon when 14, and was apprenticed to a blacksmith. He did not like the trade, and in turn bcame brickmaker, photographer, fishmonger, and then poultry and game salesman. When Mr Few first knew Swindon it was but a village. He saw the introduction of the Great Western Railway and Swindon's subsequent growth to a town with a population of 52,000.

Mr Few lived under five sovereigns, and as a lad he remembered taking part in the local celebrations of the coronation of Queen Victoria. Mr Few was one of two men who climbed the steeple of the parish church in 1851.

He is survived by his widow and five children, two sons and three daughters. Both the sons have large businesses in Swindon, and one, Mr Chrles Few, is a director of the Swindon Town football club.
Cheltenham Chronicle, October 11th 1913, p.4.

FITT, E?
Postcard publisher circa 1908. Address given as 132(?) Victoria Street, Swindon.

FORSTER, Alfred
1911 Census: Living at 22 Tennyson Street, Swindon ('photographer - apprentice').

FORSTER WILSON, William (c1870-1908)
William Forster Wilson was an Edwardian Swindon photographer and a popular 'conjuror and card manipulator'. Confusingly it seems that William sometimes spelled his middle name as 'Foster'.

1903 Kelly's: Listed at 'photographer, 55 Victoria Street'.
1907 Kelly's: 141 Victoria Road, Swindon ('photographer').
1907 NW Dir: 141 Victoria Road, Swindon ('photographer').
1908:   William dies aged 38 on January 8th 1908 at St. Margaret's Road, from 'acute consumption' - tuberculosis. He is buried at Christ Church, Swindon on January 11th 1908.

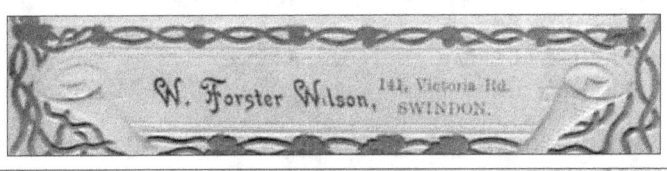

W. F. Wilson, 55 VICTORIA ST. SWINDON.

W. FORSTER WILSON'S

Specialities in Photographs

ARE THOROUGHLY UP TO DATE.

	s.	d.
ONE DOZ. CABINETS, ⅜, two positions (Two extra, mounted for framing, are given with these)	7	0
SIX CABINETS (any position) and One Enlargement mounted, 18 × 14	5	6
12 CARTE-DE-VISITS	3	6
3 CABINETS & 6 CARTE-DE-VISITS	3	6

PROOFS SUBMITTED IN ALL CASES

NO EXTRA CHARGES FOR CHILDREN.

COPYING AND ENLARGING A SPECIALITY.

ONLY ADDRESS :—

W. FORSTER WILSON,

141, VICTORIA ROAD, SWINDON.

[3259]

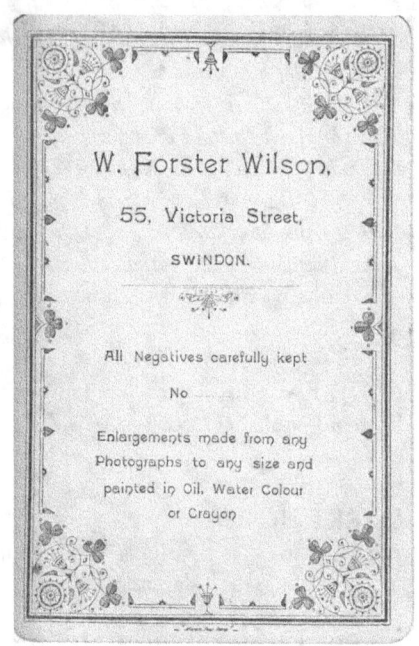

W. Forster Wilson,

55, Victoria Street,

SWINDON.

All Negatives carefully kept

No

Enlargements made from any
Photographs to any size and
painted in Oil, Water Colour
or Crayon

Swindon Advertiser, February 5th 1904.

W. Forster Wilson, 55, Victoria Street, SWINDON.

References:
COSP: 1901-1907
Pho Wilts: 55 Victoria Street, Swindon (1903).
Pho Wilts: 141 Victoria Road, Swindon (1907).
Swindon Advertiser: August 8th 1902, p.6 (conjurory and card show).
Swindon Advertiser: February 13th 1903, p.4 (conjurory and card show).
Swindon Advertiser: February 5th 1904, p.8 (advert).
Swindon Advertiser: January 10th 1908, p.5 ('Death of Mr W. Forster Wilson').

DEATH OF MR W. FORSTER WILSON.

The death took place on Wednesday at 24, St. Margaret's Road, Swindon, of Mr William Forster Wilson, who for some eight years carried on the business of a photographer at 141, Victoria Road. The deceased, who was a Londoner by birth, was only 38 years of age, and had for the past two years been in failing health. He suffered acutely from consumption, and, as far as this complaint would let him, kept on his business. Recently, however, the symptoms of the disease developed to such an extent that it became absolutely necessary for him to relinquish the photographing business.

A few weeks ago it was apparent to those about him that his strength was fast ebbing, and although during Tuesday he seemed fairly bright and conversed with his wife, he passed peacefully away shortly after ten o'clock on Wednesday morning.

During his residence in Swindon, Mr Forster Wilson made a very large circle of friends, who will deplore his death, and whose sympathies will keenly go out to the widow in her affliction.

The funeral will probably take place on Saturday.

Swindon Advertiser, January 10th 1908

| No. 875 | William Foster Wilson | 24 S. Margarets Road | January 11th 1908 | 38 Years | Charles Dams Assistant Curate |

FRY, Mr. A.

The following front page advertisement appeared in the Swindon Advertiser several times between 1863 and 1864:

PHOTOGRAPHIC PORTRAIT ROOM, KING AND QUEEN CLOSE, HIGHWORTH.

MR. A. FRY begs to inform the inhabitants of Highworth and its vicinity that he has erected a

COMMODIOUS GLASS ROOM, FOR THE PRODUCTION OF CARTES DE VISITE, AND ALL KIND OF FIRST CLASS PHOTOGRAPHIC PICTURES.

An early inspection of specimens is respectfully solicited.

Swindon Advertiser, October 19th 1863.

GOOLD, Joseph

Initially a bookseller, Joseph Goold announced the opening of his new specialized photographic studio in the North Wilts Herald in 1865. It appears that he also operated at 'The Photographic Studio, Short Hedge, Swindon' (Short Hedge later became known as Devizes Road).

References:
COSP: 1864-1865
Swindon Advertiser: December 5th 1864, p.4 (advertisement).
Swindon Advertiser: May 8th 1865 (advertisement for 3 Cricklade Street, Swindon).

1d. in the Shilling Discount off all Books, at
GOOLD'S,
BOOKSELLER, PHOTOGRAPHER, &c.,
3, CRICKLADE STREET, SWINDON.

Swindon Advertiser, December 5th 1864.

SWINDON.
GOOLD'S NEW PHOTOGRAPHIC
STUDIO, 3, CRICKLADE STREET,
Is the largest and most efficient in or near Swindon.

Album Portraits 10s. per Dozen.
Capital Glass Photographs 1s. each.

Swindon Advertiser, May 8th 1865.

GRANT, Edwin (1839–1896)

Soon after his 1861 marriage, Edwin Grant settled at 19 Gloucester Street, Faringdon, Berkshire. Around 1875 he relocated to Prospect, Old Swindon, setting up a photographic studio at 63 Prospect Place. Over the next decade the business moved into various locations around Old Swindon. An 1883 advertisement describes him as being 'from the London Stereoscopic and Photographic Company, 54, Cheapside'.

1839:	Born at Dalston, Middlesex.
1861:	Marries Elizabeth Rachel Davis.
1871 Census:	Living at 19 Gloucester Street, Faringdon ('artist').

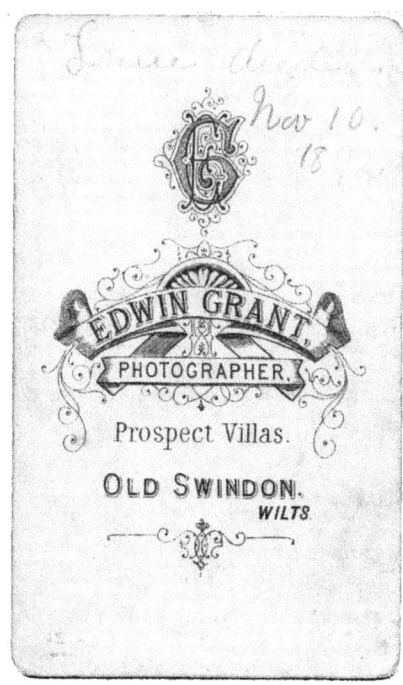
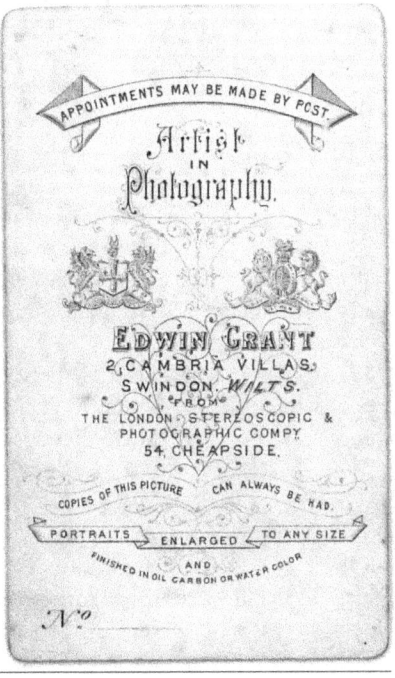

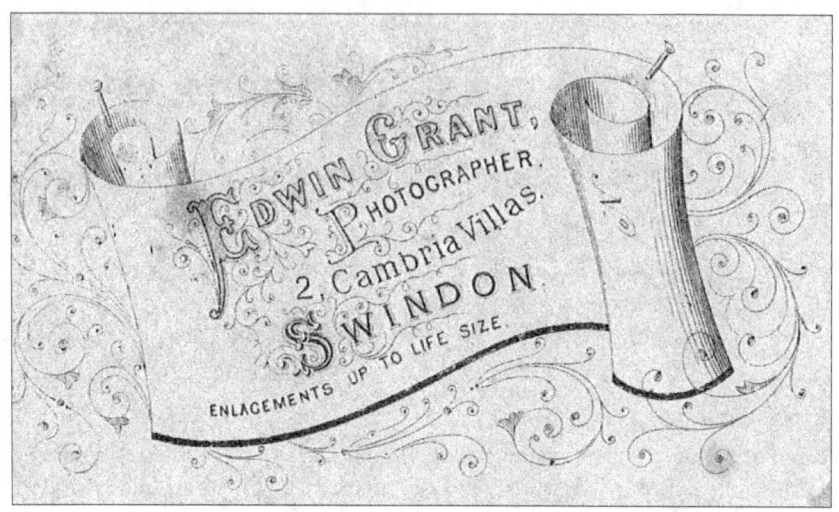

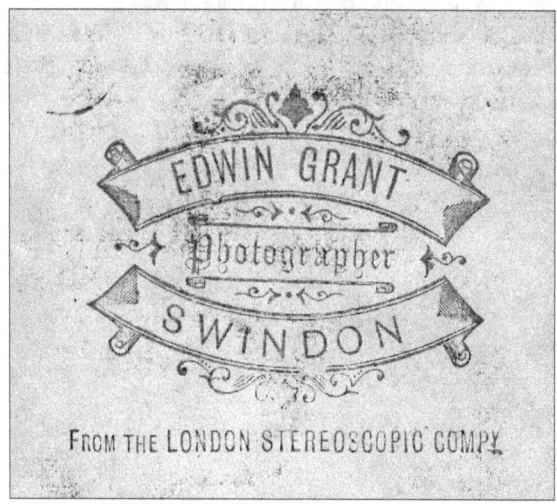

1880 Kelly's:	Listed at Prospect Lane, Swindon.
1881 Census:	63 Prospect, Old Swindon ('photographic artist').
1883 Astill's:	Described as 'est. in Faringdon eleven years and Swindon seven'.
1885:	Advertisements now give the address as Newport Street.
1890 Bennett's:	'Grant, E. photographer, 59 Prospect Place.
1896:	Edwin dies aged 57.

References:
Child, Mark: *The Swindon Book Companion* (entry pp.54-55).
COSP: 1875-1889
North Wilts Herald: April 20th 1883 (move to Marlborough Terrace, on Newport Street, Old Swindon).

Pho Wilts:	2 Prospect Villas, Swindon (1875).
Pho Wilts:	2 Cambria Villas, Prospect Lane, Swindon (1876).
Pho Wilts:	Prospect Lane, Swindon (1880).
Pho Wilts:	63 Prospect Place, Swindon (1882).
Pho Wilts:	73 Newport Street, Swindon (1885).
Pho Wilts:	16a Newport Street, Swindon (1887).

Swindon Advertiser: June 5th 1882, p.4 (article).

> **INSTANTANEOUS PHOTOGRAPHY.—We have** received from Mr Edwin Grant, photographer, 2, Cambria Villas, Swindon, two very fine specimens of instantaneous photography taken by him at the Alexandra Palace on Whit-Monday in competition for prizes offered by the Palace Company. The views, which represent scenes in the grounds of the Palace, are very effective, and we shall be pleased to hear, when the winners of the prizes are announced, that the name of our local photographer may be found among the number.

Swindon Advertiser, June 5th 1882.

GRAY, Samuel Richard (1881-1959)

Samuel Richard Gray was a Wroughton-born postcard publisher and tobacconist with his premises at Faringdon Street in Swindon. His father was a machinist in the GWR Swindon Works.

1881:	Samuel is born in Wiltshire, August 21st 1881.
1911 Census:	Living with his parents at 48 Faringdon Street, Swindon.
1915 Voters:	Samuel Richard Gray at 48 Faringdon Street, Swindon.
1939 Census:	57 Faringdon Road ('tobacconist and fancy goods dealer').
1959:	Samuel dies in Swindon in 1959, aged 78.

GREAT WESTERN PHOTOGRAPHIC COMPANY

The Great Western Photographic Company purchased the business and negatives of **William SHORT** around 1879. This was then almost immediately purchased by **Charles CANNON** in 1879. As Mark Child notes, this was Swindon's first photography business not named after an individual.

| 1880 Kelly's: | 15 Wood Street, Swindon. |

References:
Child, Mark: *The Swindon Book Companion* (entry p.55).

COSP: 1879-1880
Pho Wilts: 15 Wood Street, Old Swindon (1880).
Swindon Advertiser: November 1st 1879 (purchase by **Charles CANNON**).
Swindon Advertiser: April 3rd 1880, p.2 (advertisement).

PHOTOGRAPHY.

THE GREAT WESTERN PHOTOGRAPHIC COMPANY

Having purchased the Business lately carried on by
MR. W. SHORT,

15. WOOD STREET, SWINDON,

Are prepared to execute

PHOTOGRAPHS OF ALL KINDS,

PORTRAITS, LANDSCAPES, MANSIONS, MACHINERY, &c.

Copies of Photographs, Drawings, Engravings, & Pictures

LIFE-SIZED ENLARGEMENTS.

In Oil, Crayon, Water Colours, &c.

MICROSCOPIC OBJECTS MAGNIFIED & PHOTOGRAPHED

TRANSPARENCIES PREPARED FOR THE MAGIC LANTERN.

Full-sized and accurate copies of Engineers' and Architects' Plans.

OUT-DOOR PHOTOGRAPHS.

Family Groups, Mansions, Animals, Machinery, &c.,
Photographed, and Parties waited on at their Private
Residences by appointment.

The G.W.P. Company having purchased Mr Short's
Stock of Negatives, numbering over 12,000, are able to
supply Copies of any Photograph taken by him since 1865.

PHOTOGRAPHS TAKEN AT ANY SEASON OF THE YEAR

And in all weathers, by the newest and most highly
approved process.

THE NATURALIST DEPARTMENT.

Animal and Bird Stuffing, Taxidermy in all its
Branches, will be carried on as heretofore.

NOTE THE ADDRESS—

Opposite the KING'S ARMS HOTEL. 1277

Swindon Advertiser, Saturday 3rd April 1880.

GUGGENHEIM AND COMPANY

Following the dissolution of this company in 1902, it was continued by **Jules Sigismund GUGGENHEIM**.

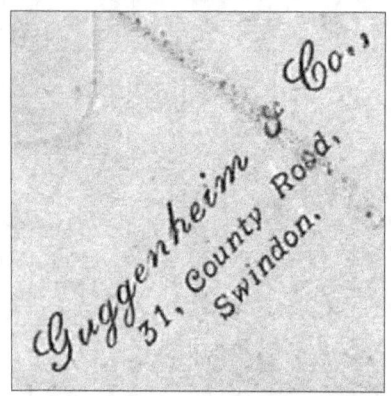
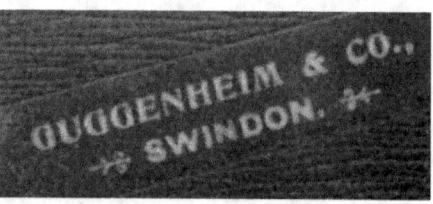

GUGGENHEIM, Jules Sigismund (1863–1938)

Jules S. Guggenheim was initially part of **GUGGENHEIM AND COMPANY**, until the company partnership was dissolved in 1902.

1863:	Jules is born at Henley.
1888:	First marriage, to Mary Ann V. Harding.
1891 Census:	Living at Regent Circus, Swindon ('photographer')
1899:	Mary Ann dies August 18th 1899, aged 33.
1899 Kelly's:	14 Regent Circus, Swindon.
1901 Census:	14 Regent Circus, Swindon ('photographer/shopkeeper') Widower.
1902:	Second marriage: Kathleen E. Clarke.
1902:	Guggenheim & Co. dissolved 'by mutual consent' on March 31st 1902.
1903 Kelly's:	Listed at 14 Regent Circus, Swindon.
1907 NW Dir:	31 County Road, Swindon.
1907 Kelly's:	31 County Road, Swindon.
1911 Kelly's:	14 County Road, Swindon.
1911 Census:	Living at 14 County Road, Swindon ('photographer').
1938:	Jules dies aged 74 while living at 145 Faringdon Road, Swindon. He is buried at Whitworth Road Cemetery on January 29th 1938.

NOTICE is hereby given, that the Partnership here-tofore subsisting between us the undersigned, Jules Sigismund Guggenheim, of 14, Regent-circus, Swindon, in the county of Wilts, and Gertrude Elizabeth Guggenheim, of Allen-road, Wolverhampton, in the county of Stafford, carrying on business as Photographers, at Number 14, Regent-circus, Swindon, in the county of Wilts, and at the City-chambers, New-street, Birmingham, in the county of Warwick, under the style or firm of "GUGGENHEIM AND COMPANY," was on the 31st day of March, 1902, dissolved by mutual consent. All debts due to and owing by the Swindon Branch of the late firm will be received and paid by the undersigned, Jules Sigismund Guggenheim, by whom the business at Swindon will in future be carried on, and all debts due to and owing by the Birmingham Branch of the late firm will be received and paid by the undersigned, Gertrude Elizabeth Guggenheim, by whom the business at Birmingham will in future be carried on.—Dated the 3rd day of April, 1902.

JULES SIGISMUND GUGGENHEIM.
GERTRUDE ELIZABETH GUGGENHEIM.

London Gazette, April 8th 1902.

References:
Child, Mark: *The Swindon Book Companion* (entry pp.56-57).
COSP: 1891-1913
London Gazette: April 8th 1902 (no.27423), p.2359.
Pho Wilts: 14 Regent Circus, Swindon (1893-1904).
Pho Wilts: 31 County Road, Swindon (1907-1909).
Pho Wilts: 14 County Road (1911).
Swindon Advertiser: August 18th 1899, p.4 (death notice for Mary Ann).
W&SHC: Photographer's Studio, 31 County Road, Swindon (1904) G24/760/2174.
W&SHC: Photographic Studio, Cambria Place (1914) G24/760/2532.

GUGGENHEIM,

Regent Circus,
Swindon.

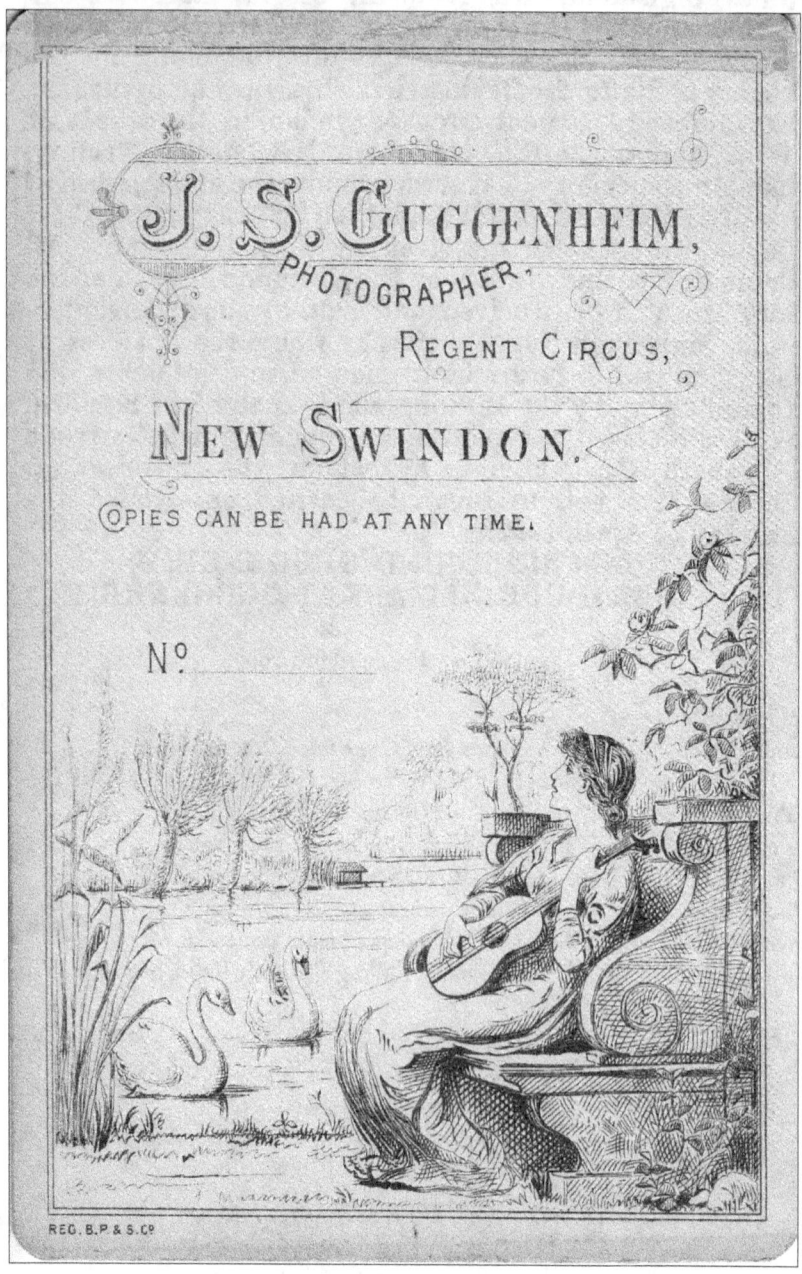

The elaborate design on the back of J.S. Guggenheim cabinet card.

HARKEY, William

The 1911 census records two photographers living as boarders at 15 Commercial Road, Swindon. William Harkey is 24 years old, born in Manchester and his occupation is given simply as 'photographer'. Fellow boarder Albert Williams is 27 years old, born in Shoreditch in London, and described as a 'photographer's assistant'. They both are living 'own account' - which indicates that they were not employers or 'working for a trade employer' (like the GWR).

HARRIS

In 1987 Swindon Museum & Art Gallery purchased a collection of circa 1000 quarter plate glass negatives of Swindon and the surrounding area (c1910-1914). Recorded as 'Mr Harris of Swindon'.

HARRISON, William Marsden

William Marsden Harrison was a 'celebrated Cornish photographer' with studios 'at Falmouth, Truro, Redruth and Helston'. His Swindon branch was based at 25, Faringdon Street, where he seems to have taken over the premises vacated by **George STONE**.

1846:	Born in Sheffield *circa* 1846.
1883 Kelly's:	Photographer, 40 Church Street, Falmouth.
1893 Kelly's:	Photographer, Penryn Street, Redruth.
1901 Census:	Living at 36 & 37 Church Street in Falmouth, Cornwall ('photographer').
1902 Kelly's:	Photographer, Penryn Street, Redruth.
1904:	Swindon premises at 25 Faringdon Street, Swindon (according to an article in the *Swindon Advertiser*).
1905:	Possibly bankruptcy proceedings.

References:
COSP: 1903-1904
Lake's Falmouth Packet & Cornwall Advertiser: April 22nd 1904, p.5 (court case).
Pho Wilts: 25 Faringdon Street, Swindon (1904).
Royal Cornwall Gazette: April 14th April 1904, p.5 (court case).
Swindon Advertiser: August 7th 1903, p.8 (takeover of George Stone's business).
Swindon Advertiser: April 22nd 1904 (court case).
West Briton & Cornwall Adv: September 30th 1912, p.3 (creditor notice).

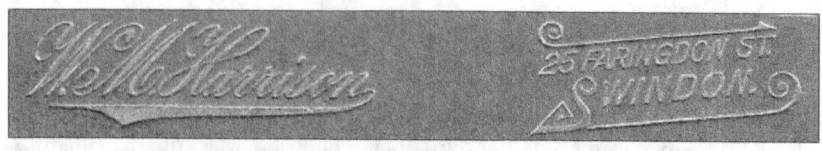

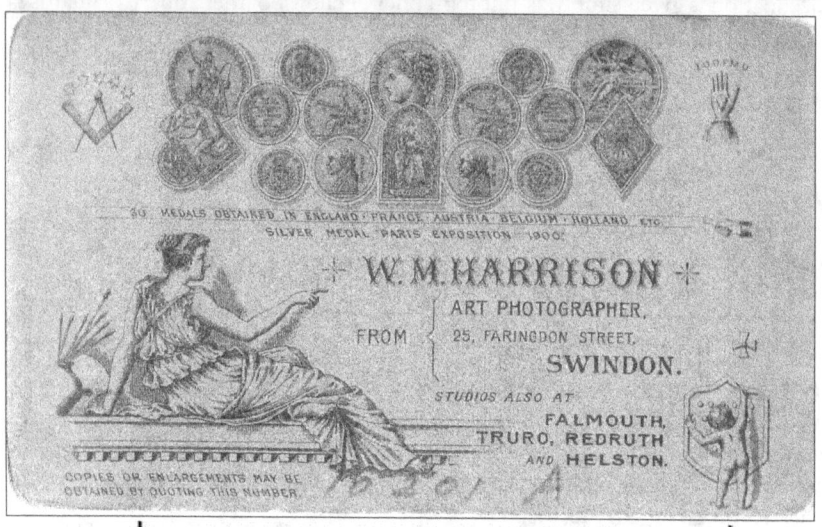

THE ESTABLISHMENT OF

Mr. GEO. STONE, PHOTOGRAPHER,

HAS BEEN TAKEN OVER BY

W. M. HARRISON,

THE

CELEBRATED CORNISH
PHOTOGRAPHER,

FALMOUTH, TRURO, REDRUTH & HELSTON,

Who has been awarded over 30 Medals for
Excellency in Photography, including one at th
Paris Exhibition of 1900.

The Business will be carried on during alterations.

Copies from Mr. STONE's negatives may be
obtained.   [2072

Swindon Advertiser, August 7th 1903.

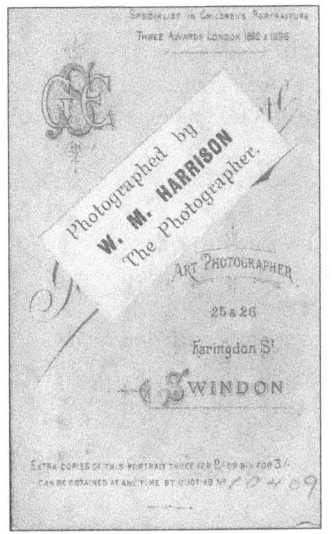

The Arrests at Falmouth.

Proceedings Withdrawn.

Before the Swindon magistrates on Monday John Harold Roberts, photographer's assistant, and his wife, Edith Blanche Roberts, both of whom are well connected at Falmouth, appeared on remand, charged with stealing a set of fish carvers, a quilt and other articles, valued at £5, and alleged to be the property of Mr. William Marsden Harrison, photographer, also of Falmouth, and who has a branch business at 25, Faringdon-street, Swindon. — Mr. H. Bevir, solicitor, represented the prosecutor, and the accused were defended by Mr. J. W. Pridham. —The defendants' solicitor asked for a further remand until Thursday, and the case stood over, both defendants being again admitted to bail.

Lake's Falmouth Packet & Cornwall Advertiser, April 22nd 1904.

HART, William (born circa 1825)

William Hart was an Oxford-born photographer with a business located on Regent Street in New Swindon circa 1881. At this time he was living as a boarder in nearby Regent Place. His fellow boarder, Walter Ainsworth, is also listed on the 1881 census as a photographer.

1881 Census: Living at 10 Regent Place ('artist & photographer').

References:
COSP: 1881

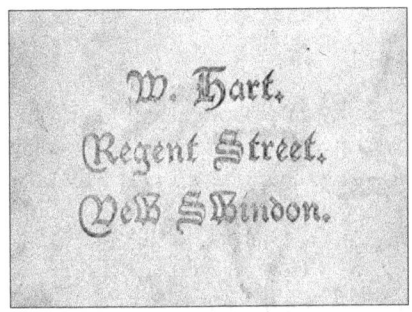

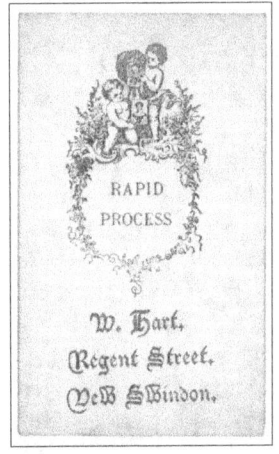

HEDGES, Frederick Ernest (1862–1955)

Frederick Hedges never took his own photographs of Bishopstone but published postcards on behalf of photographers e.g. **PROTHEROE AND SIMONS**, at the Post Office.

1862:	Born on January 14th 1862 at Buckland in Berkshire.
1896:	Marries Fannie Povey at St. Mary's Church, Bishopstone.
1901 Census:	Post Office, Bishopstone, Swindon ('grocer, baker & sub postmaster').
1911 Census:	Post Office, Bishopstone, Swindon ('shop grocer, baker & draper').
1920 Kelly's:	'Hedges, Frederick Ernest, draper, grocer, & post office'.
1939 Register:	Living at 'Fair View' Bishopstone, Swindon ('grocer – retired').
1955:	Frederick dies in Bishopstone and is buried at St. Mary's Church on January 10th 1955.

HEDGES WRIGHT LTD.

A local photography firm that ran from the 1970s onwards.

1973 Swindon Dir: Listed at Dowling Street, Swindon.

HEMMINGS, Alec William (1927-1997)

A notable amateur local photographer, whose work was published in Swindon Review and the Swindon & District Review numerous times. He was part of SALOS – Swindon Amateur Light Operatic Society (est. 1951), and he took many production and costume photographs.

HEMMINS, Francis see HEMMINS, Henry

HEMMINS, Henry (1857–1941)

In his early career Henry Hemmins worked at 'The Star Photographic Company' in Oxford, where he was a manager. He came to Swindon in 1882 and lived at Grosvenor House, 16 Victoria Street, advertising the business as **HEMMINS AND HOWELL**, portrait and landscape photographers. We have been unable to identify 'Howell'. By 1885 Henry was in business on his own in Victoria Street.

1857:	Henry is born in Eton, Buckinghamshire.
1871:	He is apprenticed to Oxford photographer Henry William Taunt for five years.
1878:	Henry marries Sarah Ann Phipps on December 26th 1878 at St. Clement, Oxford. On the marriage certificate his occupation is given as 'photographer'.
1881 Census:	Living at 15 Bullingdon Road, Oxford St. Clement, Headington ('photographer'). His lodger Richard Noyes

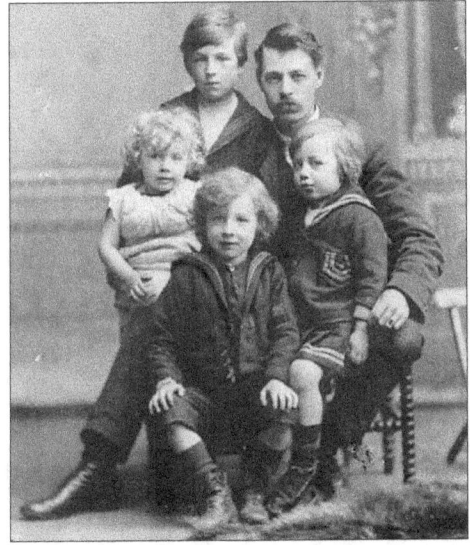
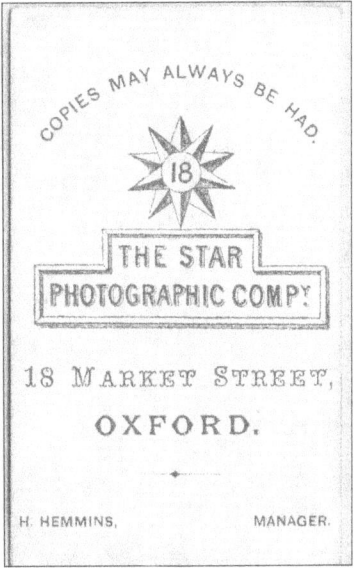

Henry Hemmins (1855-1941).

	Potter is described as working as a 'photographic printer'.
1889 Kelly's:	16 Victoria Street, Swindon.
1890 Bennett's:	Listed at Victoria Street.
1896 Kelly's:	Listed at 16 Victoria Street.
1899 Kelly's:	16 Victoria Street.
1901 Census:	Living at 16 Victoria Street (Henry and his son Francis are both recorded as 'photographer').
1903 Kelly's:	Listed at 16 Victoria Street ('photographer').
1907 Kelly's:	96 Victoria Road.
1911 Census:	Living at 96 Victoria Road ('photographer').
1915 Voters:	Living at 90 Victoria Road.
1918 Voters:	Henry and Sarah Ann living at 96 Victoria Road.
1920 Kelly's:	Listed as 'photographer, 96 Victoria Road'.
1928 S&D YB:	96 Victoria Road ('photographer').
1938 Kelly's:	96 Victoria Road.
1939 Register:	Living at 17 Upper Flat, Roxeth Green Avenue, Harrow ('retired photographer').
1941:	Henry dies aged 84 at Harrow. Middlesex and is buried at Christ Church, Swindon on October 21st 1941.

References:

Child, Mark:	*The Swindon Book Companion* (entry on p.58).
COSP:	1884-1938
Pho Wilts:	16 Victoria Street (1885-1903).
Pho Wilts:	96 Victoria Road (1907-1931).

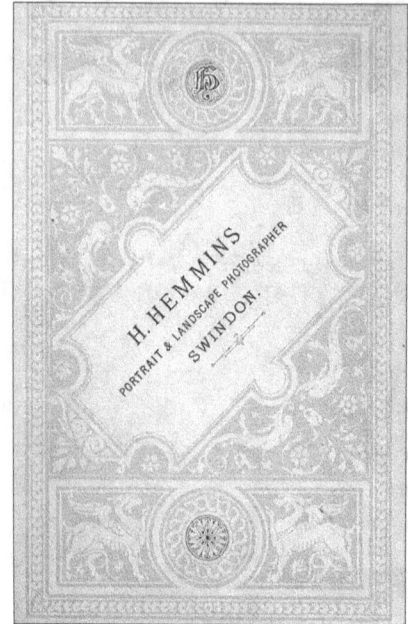
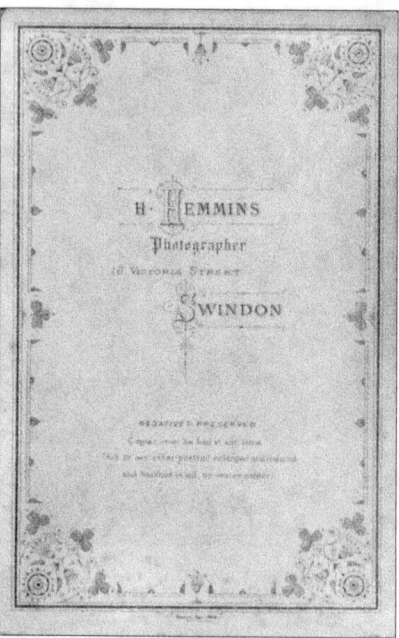

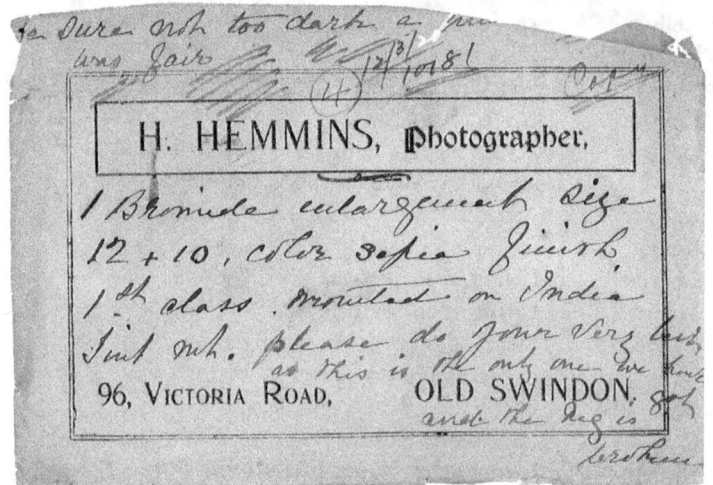

HEMMINS, T.
References:
PHOWILTS   1901   Stratton Green, Stratton St. Margaret.

HEMMINS AND HOWELL
Hemmins and Howell were 'portrait and landscape photographers' based at
Grosvenor House, Victoria Street. **Henry HEMMINS** later continued the

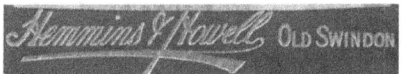

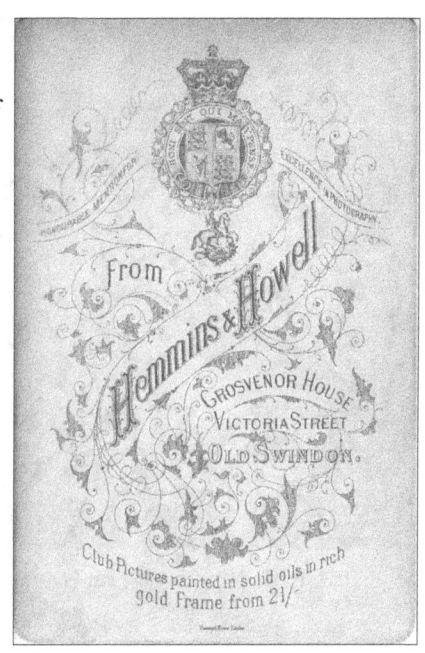

business alone, following the death of Howell.

References:

Astill's:	1883 Grosvenor House, Victoria Street, Swindon.
COSP:	1882-1884
Pho Wilts:	1883-1885

HIGGINS, R.A.
References:

COSP   1921-1922

HILL, William Charles Bramwell (1897–1963)
A Stratton-born journalist, lecturer, poet, and Primitive Methodist preacher. William was also President of the Christian Endeavour Union. His family name does appear to be 'Hill' but he often used a hyphenated form of his name: 'Bramwell-Hill'.

1897:	Born September 12th 1897 at Stratton St. Margaret. Son of William Henry Hill, who ran the Cart & Wagon Works business.
1901 Census:	Stratton Cross Roads ('coach builder & shoeing smith').
1911 Census:	Living at the Laurels, Swindon Road, Lower Stratton, Stratton St. Margaret ('shoeing & general smith, coach builder').
1925:	William marries Norah M. Barnes.
1939 Register:	Living at 125 Oxford Road, Swindon ('journalist, preacher & lecturer professional').
1963:	William dies in Swindon aged 65.

References:
Banbury Advertiser: March 8th 1928, p.2 (article).
Hill, W. Bramwell: *Wistful Wiltshire and other poems* (1954).
Lichfield Mercury: April 14th 1939, p.8 (article with a portrait photograph).

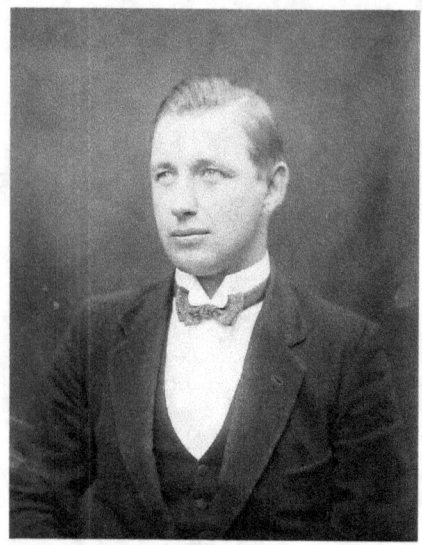

William Charles Bramwell Hill (1897–1963)

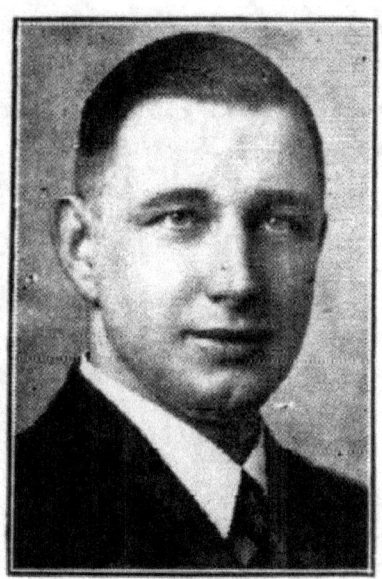

MR. W. BRAMWELL HILL

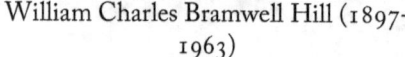

Published by: W. & N. M. Bramwell-Hill, Stratton Park Post Office and Stores, SWINDON, (Foreign).

HODGE, Frederick W.

Frederick Hodge was a local photographer based at 100 Cricklade Road, Swindon.

1949 S&D YB:	100 Cricklade Road, Swindon.
1951 S&D YB:	100 Cricklade Road, Swindon.
1952 S&D YB:	Listed under 'photographers' at 100 Cricklade Road, Swindon.

HOOD, Josiah Charles 'Clarance' (1865–1952)

Although at birth his middle name was given as Charles, for unknown reasons Josiah took to using the name 'Clarance' on his *carte de visite* and Cabinet cards. Like **William HOOPER**, Clarance also produced postcards of the crowds at the GWR Juvenile Fete, circa 1908. Swindon Museum & Art Gallery have 6 paintings by J. Hood in their local art collection, which were donated to the museum by James E. 'Raggy' Powell (1849-1930).

1865:	Born November 26th 1865, in Stratton St. Margaret.
1881 Census:	Living at Stratton Green, Stratton St. Margaret ('painter').
1889:	A poem by Clarance called 'In Memoriam' appears in the Swindon Advertiser to commemorate the death of James 'Jimmy' Munro (January 6th 1889), a STFC player

regarded as Swindon's first professional.

1891 Census:	Upper Stratton, Stratton St. Margaret ('coach painter GWR').
1901 Census:	Neate House, Dores Lane, Stratton St. Margaret ('photo artist').
1903 Kelly's:	Listed at 25 Oxford Terrace, Swindon ('photographer').
1907 NW DIR:	25 Oxford Terrace, Swindon.
1911 Kelly's	25 Oxford Terrace, Swindon.
1911 Census:	Living at Dores Lane, Stratton St. Margaret ('photographer').
1919:	He marries Miss Elsie Olive Cox.
1939 Register:	Living at 471 Cricklade Road ('sign writer ex-photographer: incapacitated')
1952:	Josiah dies in Swindon aged 86 and is buried at Whitworth Road, Cemetery, Swindon on July 26th 1952.

References:
COSP:	1900-1913
Pho Wilts:	Bath Terrace, Swindon (1901).
Pho Wilts:	Oxford Terrace, Swindon (1903-1911).
Swindon Advertiser:	January 6th 1889.
Art UK:	https://artuk.org/discover/artists/hood-j-(6 paintings by Hood)

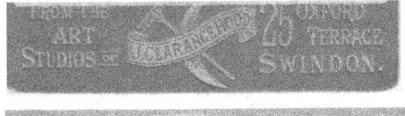
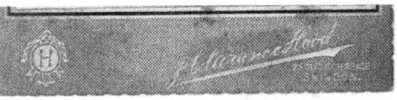
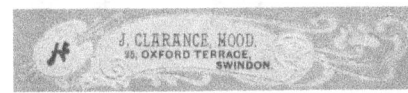
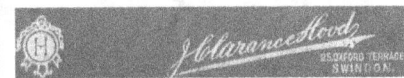

HOOPER, William (1864–1955)

Born on January 24th 1864 at Windrush, Gloucestershire, William Hooper came to Swindon in 1882 and was employed in GWR Swindon Works. He married Mary Jane Stroud at the Baptist Tabernacle on 3rd May 1890. Whilst at work he suffered a serious accident resulting in amputation at the knee in 1886. He recovered and continued to work for the GWR until 1902 when he was dismissed on medical grounds. From then on he was to become Swindon's most famous photographer.

As result of leaving the GWR he took up photography in a professional capacity – a venture which began in the late 1890s through the efforts of his brother-in-law **Thomas RICHARDS**. William began working from his home at 22 Merton Street, but his business soon outgrew that property, so he acquired his first studio at 2 Market Street around 1901/2, before moving in 1906 to

HOOPERS, ◎ Photographic . . Artists, ...

THE STUDIO, CROMWELL ST., SWINDON.

PICTORIAL POST CARDS OF THE NEIGHBOURHOOD.

☞ Special Attention given to Copying and Enlarging Old and Faded Photographs without injury to the Original.

BEST RESULTS GUARANTEED

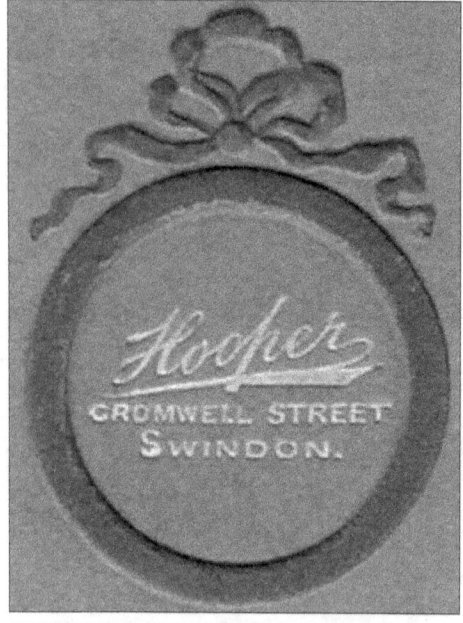

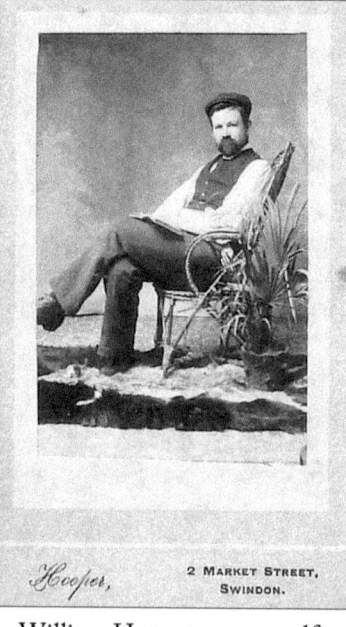

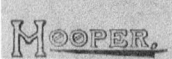

William Hooper: a 1902 self portrait.

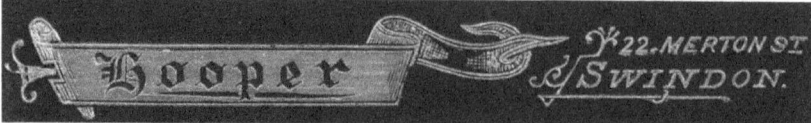

his most famous location at 6 Cromwell Street ('The Day and Electric Light Studio').

Business continued in Cromwell Street until around 1921, when William retired and Plymouth photographer **Fred C. PALMER** purchased the business. William died on the January 4th 1955 at 10 London Street, and was buried at Radnor Street Cemetery, Swindon. The copyright to the Hooper photographic collection is currently managed by his descendent Paul A. Williams.

1864:	William is born January 24th 1864 at Windrush.
1890:	Marries Mary Jane Stroud on May 3rd 1890 at the Baptist Tabernacle.
1891 Census:	9 Oxford Street, Swindon (recorded as 'labourer railway factory').
1901 Census:	10 Market Street, Swindon ('engine fitter / labourer').
1903 Kelly's:	Listed at 2 Market Street, Swindon ('photographer').
1907 Kelly's:	6 Cromwell Street, Swindon.
1907 NW Dir:	6 Cromwell Street, Swindon.
1911 Kelly's:	6 Cromwell Street, Swindon.
1911 Census:	Living at 6 Cromwell Street ('photographer portrait and landscape').

Swindon Advertiser, July 6th 1906, p.6

DRIVING CATTLE THROUGH THE STREETS.

To the Editor of the "Swindon Advertiser."

Sir.—I ask your assistance in ventilating what I consider a serious danger to the public of Swindon, viz., the practice of butchers and others in driving infuriated animals through the town without having same under proper control. It is quite time some measures were taken by the authorities to prevent a recurrence of such an incident as happened to myself and others to-day. At 5-30 to-day (Monday) I was engaged taking a photograph of the new block of shops at the corner of Curtis Street and Commercial Road. While I had my head covered by the focussing cloth, I heard shouts behind me. On looking round to discover the cause of the noise, I saw a cow about three or four paces off, with her head down in the act of charging me In the effort to save myself and camera—a 12in. by 10in., and rather a heavy one—I fell, severely bruising my knee. Before I could recover myself and get away, the animal turned to charge me a second time. This was prevented by one of the attendants striking it a severe blow or two on the nose.

After this the infuriated beast charged straight at Mr C. W. James, bootmaker, Commercial Road. In trying to save himself, he slipped and fell on his back, the animal leaping over him. The fall evidently saved him from being gored. I am informed that a lady had been driven into a shop to escape the beast just previously.

I think, sir, as it is such a short time since Miss Stone was fatally injured through a similar cause in this town, it is quite time something was done to prevent occurrences of this kind.

Yours faithfully,
WILLIAM HOOPER.
Cromwell Street, Swindon, April 29th, 1907.

Swindon Advertiser,
May 3rd 1907.

1920 Kelly's:	Listed as 'photographer, 6 Cromwell Street'.
1939 Register:	142 Kingsdown Road ('portrait & landscape photograph – retired').
1955:	William dies in Swindon on January 4th 1955.
1955:	Hooper's estate notice appears in the *London Gazette*, January 28th 1955.

References:

Child, Mark:	*The Swindon Book* (entry on p.128).
COSP:	1901-1921
London Gazette:	January 28th 1955 (estate notice).
Pho Wilts:	2 Market Street, Swindon (1903).
Pho Wilts:	6 Cromwell Street, Swindon - 'The Studio' (1907-1919).
Swindon Advertiser:	June 29th 1906, p.4 (an angry letter by Hooper responding to accusations that he faked his photograph of a lighting flash at Regent Circus).
Swindon Advertiser:	July 6th 1906, p.6 (an advertisement announcing that Hooper had won prizes for two of his photographs: (1) the aftermath of the Swindon tram disaster and (2) 'most unique photograph of a flash of lightning').
Swindon Advertiser:	May 3rd 1907, p.5 (letter by Hooper about being attacked by a cow!).
Swindon Advertiser:	May 3rd 1947, p.1 (Hooper's 57th wedding anniversary).
Swindon Advertiser:	September 29th 1979 (biographical article).
Swindon Heritage:	Spring 2013 (no.1), pp.15-17 ('William Hooper: a life through a lens').
Swindon Society:	*Swindon: A Sixth Selection* (Chapter 6, pp.81-93).
Williams, Paul A.:	*The Life & Times of William Hooper: Swindon Photographer* (Swindon: 2007 & 2010).
Williams, Paul A:	*William Hooper's Swindon & District: a portrait in old photographs and old picture postcards.* Vol. 1 (Seaford: S.B. Publications, 1991).
Williams, Paul A:	*William Hooper's Swindon & District : a portrait in old photographs and old picture postcards.* Vol. 2 (Seaford: S.B. Publications, 1993).

HUFF, John William

John William Huff took over the photographic business of **Alexander Alfred BETTS** at 59 Prospect in Old Swindon. His business was itself taken over by **Henry DOBBINSON** circa 1900. See also **WILSON AND HUFF**.

1899 Kelly's:	59 Prospect, Swindon.

References:

COSP	1898-1899
PHOWILTS	59 Prospect, Swindon (1898-1899).

HUGHES, James (b. 1851)

1851:	Born in Faringdon, Berkshire.
1878:	Marries Sarah Larissa Wheeler.
1881 Census:	51 Bridge Street, Swindon ('printer's manager').
1891 Census:	Bridge Street, Swindon ('printer, local preacher').
1901 Census:	51 Bridge Street, Swindon ('printer bookseller').
1903 Kelly's:	Listed at 51 Bridge Street ('printer & stationer').
1911 Census:	Living at Clarendon Villa, 22 Drove Road, Swindon ('retired printer & stationer').

HULLIN, Thomas (1870–1953)

The 51 Fleet Street address of newsagent Thomas Hullin is sometimes given as 'Tram Centre'.

1870:	Thomas is born in Wales.
1891 Census:	White Street, Swansea ('newspaper clerk').
1896:	Marries Mabel Pannett at St. James Church, Swansea on December 2nd 1896.
1900:	T. Hullin of 51 Fleet Street is mentioned in the Swindon Advertiser as an agent for the Wiltshire Times.
1901 Census:	Stationers shop, 51 Fleet Street Swindon ('shopkeeper stationer').
1903 Kelly's:	Listed 51 Fleet Street ('stationer & news agent').
1911 Census:	Living at 53 Fleet Street, Swindon ('stationer'). Mabel is recorded as 'assisting in business'.
1920 Kelly's:	Listed as 'stationer & news agent, 53 Fleet Street'.
1939 Register:	Living at 791 Fulham Road, Fulham ('off licensee').
1953:	Thomas dies aged 83.

References:

COSP:	c1910

HUMPHREY, Frederick

Frederick Humphrey was a postcard publisher and photographer at Maxwell Street, Swindon.

1873:	Fredrick is born in Islington, London.
1901:	He marries Elizabeth (who was born in Swindon).

1911 Census: 45 Victor Road, Finsbury Park, Islington, London ('photographer').

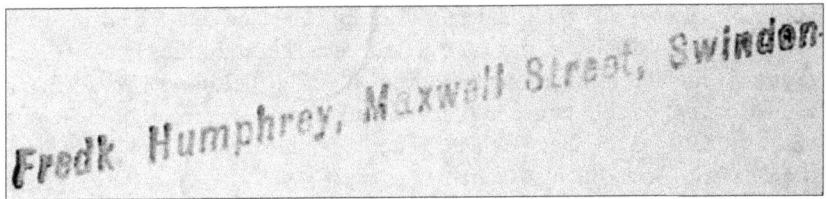

HUMPHRIES, William
1911 Census: Living at 54 York Road, Swindon. Described as 'photographer – assistant').

HUNT, E.S.
Very little is known about this photographer. We have found a Sidney Hunt listed at 14 Princes Street on the 1915 voters list.

References:
1915 Voters: Sidney Hunt of 14 Princes Street.

COSP   c1910

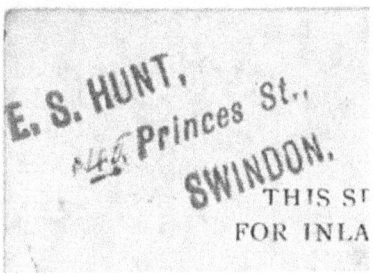

INSIGHT PHOTOGRAPHY
A 1970s Swindon photography firm.

IRELAND, Walter Charles Jonas (1894-1978)
A number of postcards are marked as 'Published by D. Last. Post Office, Chiseldon'.

1894:   Walter is born December 16th 1894.
1895:   Baptised February 17th 1895.
1911 Census: Living at 4 Page Street, Swindon ('apprentice photographer').
1921:   Marries Florence E. Haines in Swindon.
1939 Register: Living at 34 Brynards Hill Road, Wootton Bassett ('railway clerk').
1978:   Walter dies in Swindon.

JEFFERIES, Charles John (c1852-1899)

Charles J. Jefferies came to Swindon from London around 1880, leaving the Bank of England to work for the Great Western Railway as a draughtsman. He eventually became their Chief Photographer, responsible for many of the photographs on display in their railway carriages. He was killed in September 1899 in a horrific accident on the railway lines. At the time he was living at 283 Cricklade Road in Gorse Hill. He was a Forester - Secretary of the 'Gorse Hill Pride' A.O.F. ('Ancient Order of Foresters'). His funeral took place at St. Barnabas in Gorse Hill, in a 'drenching storm'.

References:
Swindon Advertiser: September 29th 1899, p.6 (accident report).
Swindon Advertiser: October 6th 1899, p.5 (report on his funeral).
Swindon Advertiser: October 20th 1899, p.4 (election of new A.O.F. Secretary).

JOHNSON, Richard William (1873–1926)

1873:	Richard is born in London.
1890/1891:	Marries Annie Matilda Baker.
1907:	Appears to have moved to Supply Cottage, Hinton, living in the village until at least 1915.
1907 Kelly's:	Little Hinton ('grocer').
1911 Census:	Little Hinton, Swindon ('photographer').
1915:	The Johnson family move on to Lydiard Millicent.
1926:	Richard dies on March 18th 1926 at Lydiard Millicent, and is buried on March 23rd 1926 at Little Hinton.

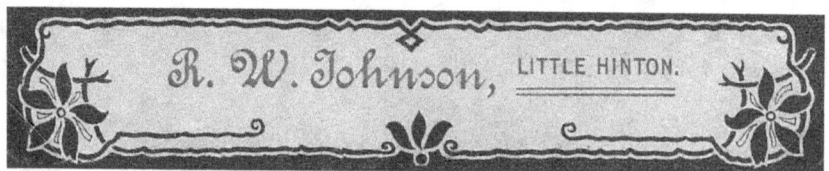

R. W. Johnson, LITTLE HINTON.

KERSLAKE, Minnie, Louisa Edith [née Cowley] (1874–1924)

Some of Minnie Kerslake's advertisements give her address as 'The Central Art Gallery, Tram Centre, Gorse Hill, Swindon'.

1874:	Born in London.
1896:	Marries George Kerslake.
1901 Census:	Living at 20 Gooch Street, Swindon.
1911 Census:	85 Cricklade Road, Gorse Hill, Swindon ('picture frame dealer').
1918 Voters:	George and Minnie living at 85 Cricklade Road.
1920 Kelly's:	Listed as 'picture frame maker, at 85 Cricklade Road, and

	53b Fleet Street'.
1924:	Minnie dies in Swindon aged 50.

References:
PHOWILTS   Tram Centre, Gorse Hill (1917).

KING, George (1834–1872)

George King was born in 1834 at Hastings in Sussex. By the age of 16, he was already working as a photographer. In 1866 he then went into partnership with **Edward BUTLER** in Swindon, forming the photographic firm **BUTLER & KING**. His earliest advertisements describe his service as 'portraits, in a superior style, taken in a room'.

1834:	Born at Hastings, Sussex.
1851 Census	Short Hedge, Swindon, with his aunt Sarah Tuck.
1861 Census:	Short Hedge, Swindon ('photographer') with aunt Sarah Tuck.
1867 Kelly's:	Devizes Road, Swindon.
1868 Loyal:	Devizes Road, Swindon.
1869 SA&D:	Devizes Road, Swindon ('photographer').
1871 Census:	8 Devizes Road, Swindon ('photographer') with aunt Sarah Tuck.
1872:	George dies, aged just 38.

References:
Child, Mark: *The Swindon Book Companion* (entry p.68).

A FREEHOLD BUILDING SITE, situate in the Devizes Road, Swindon, Wilts, containing about 42 perches, and having a frontage to the Street of 75 feet, formerly the property of the late Mr GEORGE KING, Photographer, comprising :—

Swindon Advertiser, June 27th 1891.

G. KING,
PHOTOGRAPHER,
SHORT-HEDGE, SWINDON.

Portraits, in a Superior Style, taken in a Room.

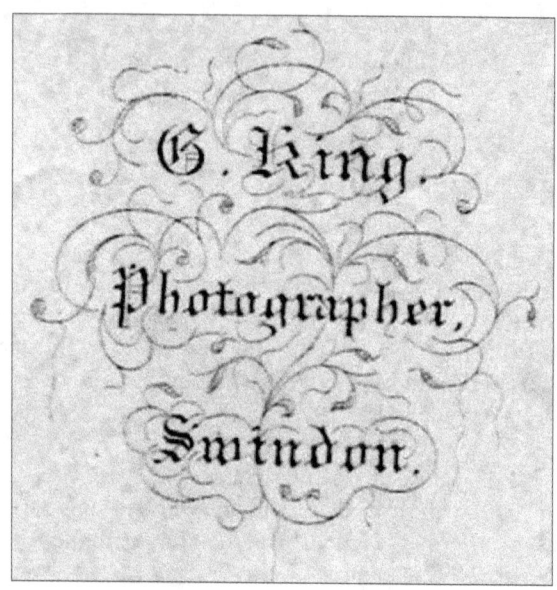

COSP:	1859-1876.
Pho Wilts:	Devizes Road, Swindon (1865-1872).
Pho Wilts:	Regent Street, Swindon (1872).
Pho Wilts:	1 Regent Street, Swindon (1875).
Swindon Advertiser:	September 10th 1860, p.1 (advertisement).
Swindon Advertiser:	December 16th 1861, p.1 (advertisement).
Swindon Advertiser:	September 22nd 1873, p.4 (witness in court case concerning mistreatment of a horse by blacksmith George Howard).
Swindon Advertiser:	June 27th 1891 (freehold notice).

KING, J.R.
Very little is known about this Victorian Swindon photographer.

References:
COSP   1880s

KING AND DODSON
A Victorian photography partnership based at Devizes Road, Old Swindon.

When **Edward BUTLER** left **BUTLER AND KING** he was replaced by **Zephaniah DODSON**.

References:
COSP: 1869-1870
Pho Wilts: Devizes [Road?], Old Swindon (1869-1870).

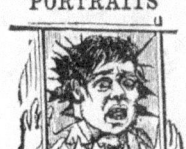

PORTRAITS

KING & DODSON, PHOTOGRAPHERS, DEVIZES ROAD, SWINDON,

FRAMED & GLAZED,
One Shilling.

Invite attention to their

CARTE DE VISITE PORTRAITS AND VIGNETTES,

EITHER PLAIN, TINTED, OR FINISHED IN COLORS.

Paintings, Engravings, Plans, Drawings, and Photographs Copied or Restored. Landscape and Architectural Photography. Machinery and Engineering Works Photographed. Portraits for Lockets, Brooches, Rings, &c.

CARTE DE VISITE PORTRAITS TAKEN ALL WEATHERS.

The Studio is well Warmed during the Winter Months.

RESIDENCES, &c., PHOTOGRAPHED.

Address : KING & DODSON, Devizes Road, Swindon.

KING, Thomas (1851 - ?)
After a career in the GWR, Thomas King took on the Tower Stores in Wroughton High Street, which later became the premises of **J.W. DECENT**.

1851:   Born at Wroughton.
1861 Census: Wroughton Village, Wroughton ('scholar').
1871 Census: High Street, Wroughton ('boiler smith').
1875:   Marries Caroline Webb of Guernsey Island on October 2nd 1875 at Bristol.
1891 Census: Living at Fosbury Cottages, Baker Mill Lane, Wroughton ('GWR boiler smith').
1901 Census: 136 Great Knolly Street, Reading ('railway boiler smith').
1911 Census: 52 George Street, Reading ('boiler smith').

References:
Wroughton LHG: *Wroughton History*, Part 2, pp.117-118 (overview of Tower
                  Stores).

Published by Mr. Tom King, The Tower Stores, Wroughton.

LANG, R.

R. Lang was a newsagent and stationer of 33 Fleet Street, Swindon, who published postcards *circa* 1918.

Published by R. Lang, Newsagent & Stationer.
33 Fleet Street, Swindon.

LAST, Daniel (1847–1930)

1847:	Born 2nd August 1847 at Shipdham, Norfolk.
1897:	Marries Sarah Annie Cannon of Swindon.
1901 Census:	Post Office, Chiseldon ('draper'). Wife acting as 'sub post mistress'.
1911 Census:	Post Office, Chiseldon ('general dealer'). Wife acting as 'sub post mistress'.
1930:	Daniel dies aged 83.

LILLEY, Thomas Lambert (1855–1935)

Thomas Lambert LILLEY had a studio at 'The Blossoms' in Bournemouth and later at 17 Commercial Road, Swindon.

1855:	Born at Scarborough.
1881 Census:	6, Crowther Terrace, Holdenhurst, Christchurch ('photographer')
1886:	Marries Alice Maud Tall.
1899 Kelly's:	Listed at 17 Commercial Road, Swindon.
1901 Census:	152 Northam Road, Southampton ('shop keeper – dairy').
1935:	Thomas dies aged 79.

References:
COSP:	1896-1899
Pho Wilts:	Commercial Road, Swindon (1898-1899).

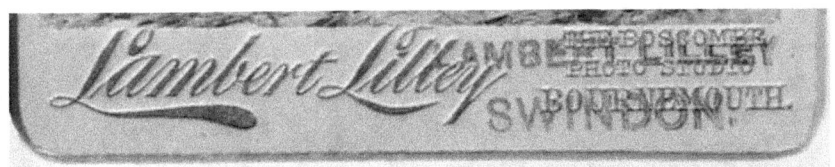

*

LONDON FINE ART COMPANY

This may be the Swindon side of a Gloucestershire photography firm owned by Jabez Skingle, who had premises at Barton Street, Gloucester. His career was abruptly curtailed in July 1900 when he was arrested in Bristol and charged with 'perpetrating the abominable crime' of 'gross indecency'. Jabez failed to appear in court, went on the run and a warrant was issued for his arrest. He next appears 13 years later, on the passenger list for a 1913 voyage from Liverpool to New York aboard the S.S. Celtic. He ended up living in Philadelphia.

References:
Bristol Mercury: July 11th 1900, p.2 (court case).
Calendar of Prisoners:Bristol, July 5th 1900.
COSP   1894–1895
Gloucester Citizen: June 18th 1890, p.2 (advertisement).
Passenger list: New York, March 2nd 1913.
Police Gazette: August 10th 1900, p.2.

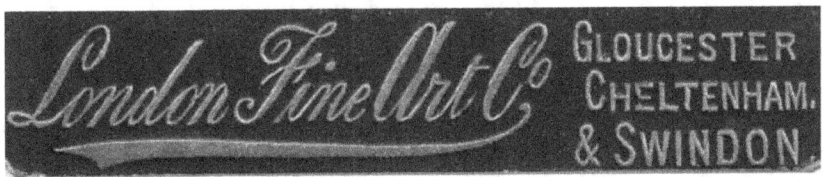

LUMKIN, Lucy (1884 - ?)

Lucy Lumkin was a Gorse Hill newsagent who published postcards from her premises at 88 Cricklade Road, Swindon.

1884:   Lucy Richens was born on December 26th 1884.
1920:   Marries Reginald Anthony Lumkin (b. 1896) in Swindon.
1920 Kelly's: Listed as 'news agent, 88 Cricklade Road'.
1939 Register: Living at 88 Cricklade Road, Swindon ('newsagent').

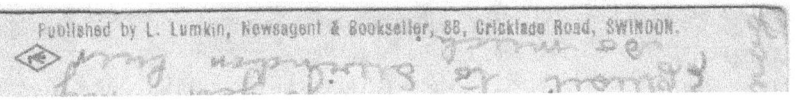

MARCHBANK AND CO.

Taken from a notice published in the Swindon Advertiser (May 3rd 1858, p.1). The address is given as 'Top of Victoria Street, Swindon':

MARCHBANK & Co.,
PHOTOGRAPHIC ARTISTS,
TOP OF VICTORIA STREET, SWINDON.

RESPECTFULLY announce to the Nobility, Clergy, and Gentry of SWINDON and its Vicinity, that their PORTRAIT GALLERYS are now open for a short time only, where PHOTOGRAPHIC COLLODION PORTRAITS are taken daily from 10 A.M. till 4 P.M.

These Pictures excel all others in beauty and softness of tint, while for minuteness of detail and life-like Portraiture they stand unrivalled.

Sunshine not required in this Improved Process.

ANCIENT AND MODERN PICTURES RESTORED

April, 1858.

Swindon Advertiser, May 3rd 1858, p.1.

MAYBURY, Alfred [Fred] & Sons (1851–1913)

Alfred 'Fred' Maybury was a prolific printer and postcard manufacturer. His son Alfred Percy Maybury, (born 1880 in Birmingham) assisted in the business.

1851:	Born in 1851.
1879:	Marries Alice (Cecelia) H. Malpass.
1891 Census:	Great Charles Street, Birmingham ('printer and book binder').
1901 Census:	76 Eastcott Hill, Swindon ('printer / shopkeeper').
1903 Kelly's:	Regent Circus, Swindon.
1907 Kelly's:	13 Regent Circus, Swindon.
1911 Census:	Living at 76 Eastcott Hill, Swindon.
1913:	Alfred dies aged 62.
1920 Kelly's:	Listing for Maybury & Sons, at 13 Regent Circus.
1956:	Son Alfred Percy dies aged 76.

MAYLOTT, Leonard Cousins (1891–1971)

Leonard Cousins Maylott was the founder of one of Swindon's longest running and most prolific photography studios. Note that Faringdon Street is just the original name for Faringdon Road.

1891:	Leonard is born on December 31st 1891.
1911 Census:	Living at 25 Lorne Street, Swindon ('photographer')
1922:	Marries Emma A. Butler.
1923 Kelly's:	25 Faringdon Road, Swindon (printed as 'Leonard Charles').

1926 S&D YB:	25 Faringdon Street, Swindon.
1931 S&D YB:	31 Faringdon Road, Swindon.
1939 Register:	Living at 31 Faringdon Road, Swindon ('photographer – master').
1948 S&D YB:	31 Faringdon Road & 22a Wood Street, Swindon.
1951 PO Dir:	31 Faringdon Road, Swindon.
1953 S&D YB:	31 Faringdon Road, Swindon.
1965 Swindon Dir:	Maylott Studios Ltd., 31 Faringdon Road.
1970 Swindon Dir:	31 Faringdon Road, Swindon.
1971:	Leonard dies aged 80, and is buried at Christ Church, Swindon on June 4th 1971.

References:

| COSP: | 1922-1974 |
| Pho Wilts: | 31 Faringdon Road, Swindon (1923-1939). |

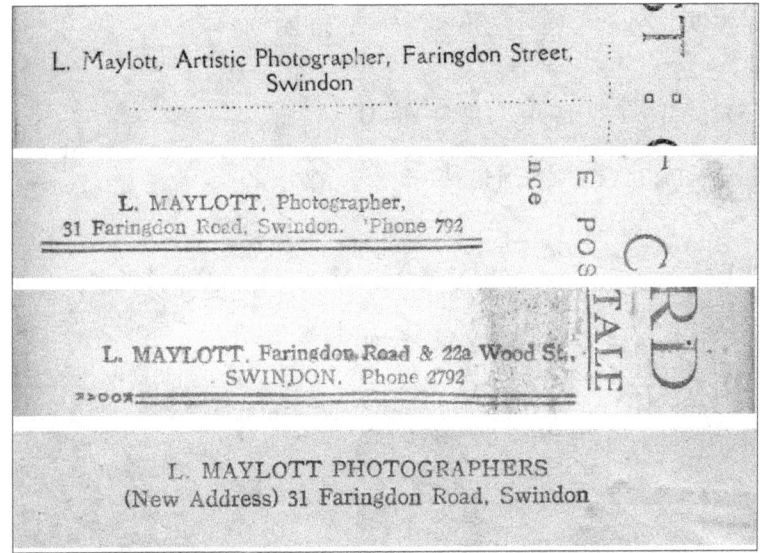

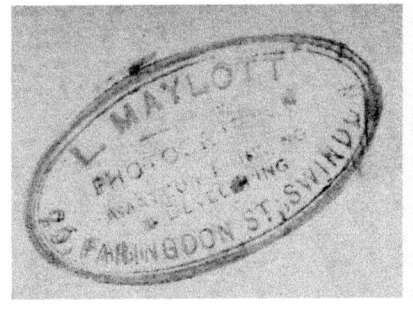
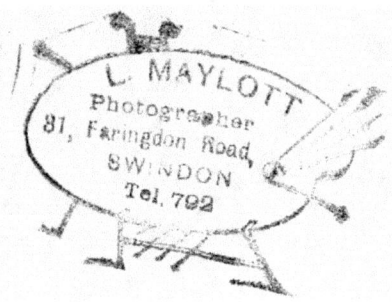

METZGER, B.

Found on an early postcard: 'B. Metzger, [18] Glo'ster [Gloucester] Terrace, Swindon'.

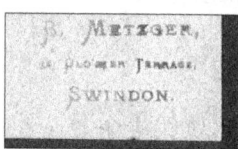

MORSES LTD.

This major New Swindon shop was opened by Levi Lapper Morse in 1878. It sold 'parlour, bed-room & general household furniture, hardware, kitchen utensils and small articles'. Morses was only the second shop of its kind in Swindon, after William McIlroy's. The store was closed in early 1970's after which W.H. Smith acquired the premises in 1973.

Morses Ltd, is listed under 'photographers' in the 1950s editions of the Swindon & District Directory and Year Book, so we can presume they offered some form of in-house service.

References:
Mark Child: *The Swindon Book* (entry on page 182).

NASH, Alfred William (1893–1944)

Alfred W. Nash was a photographer with premises at 'Piccadilly Studio' on Draycott Road in the Chiseldon Camp.

1893:	Alfred is born on June 29th 1893.
1911 Census:	93 Sultan Road, Mile End, Portsmouth ('chemist apprentice').
1922:	Marries May B. Harris.
1939 Register:	Keeping Gate House, New Forest, Hampshire ('retail dispensing chemist & photographer's assistant').
1944:	Alfred dies aged 51.

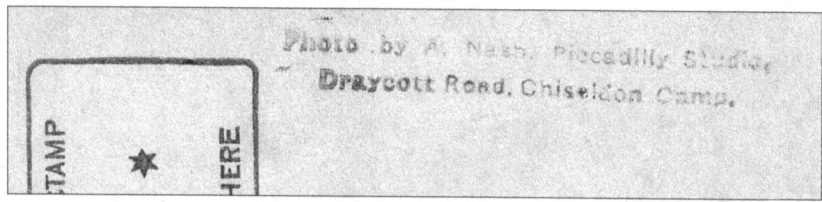

NEWSOME, Hector Edmund (1879–1961)

Hector Edmund Newsome was an Edwardian postcard publisher and stationer, with his premises at 60 Wellington Street, Swindon.

1879:	Born in Bath on August 8th 1879.

1891 Census:	Living at Spring Gardens, Swindon.
1904:	Marries Lilian Weston Browne.
1911 Census:	13 Rock Road, Midsomer Norton, Bath ('Insurance Agent').
1939 Register:	Living at 115 Cheney Manor Road, Swindon ('assistant warehouse mgr. GWR').
1961:	Hector dies aged 82, and is buried at Whitworth Road Cemetery, Swindon on November 22nd 1961.

NORTH WILTS FIELD AND CAMERA CLUB
The long-running local photography society linked to the Royal Photographic Society.

NUNNEY, Frederick (1888–1961)

1888:	Born in 1888 at Burford in Oxfordshire.
1901 Census:	78 High Street, Marlborough ('printer's apprentice')
1911:	Marries Florence Basson.
1911 Census:	190 Victoria Road, Swindon ('Pearl Insurance Agent').
1916:	Death of his wife Florence.
1930:	Remarries to Dorothy S. Rowland.
1939 Register:	2 Searle Street, Crediton, Devon ('Insurance Collector').
1961:	Frederick dies in 1961.

References:

COSP:	1907-1908
Pho Wilts:	London Road, Marlborough (1907).

OSTLER, William Nelson (1885–1970)
A Swindon-born photographer with premises in Regent Street.

1885:	William is born in Swindon on October 13th 1885.
1911 Census:	Living at 15 Jennings Street, Swindon ('photographer').
1913 Kelly's:	30 Regent Street, Swindon.
1915 Kelly's:	30 Regent Street, Swindon.
1915:	Marries Madeline Hart.
1920 Kelly's:	Listed as 'photographer, 30 Regent Street'.
1920 NW Dir:	Listed as 'photographer'.
1926 S&D YB:	30 Regent Street, Swindon.
1928 S&D YB:	30 Regent Street ('photographer').
1939 Register:	90 Abingdon Road, Oxford ('photographer – retired').
1970:	William dies in Swindon.

References:
COSP: 1912-1928
Pho Wilts: 30 Regent Street, Swindon (1915-1927).

PALMER, Fred Christian (1866–1941)

Fred C. Palmer's father, William Eastmann Palmer, became a photographer in the 1860's. He had twelve children and of his seven sons, at least five trained as photographers – including Frederick Christian Palmer. They operated in Plymouth as 'William Eastmann Palmer & Sons'. Then sometime around 1921 F.C. Palmer purchased the studio at 6 Cromwell Street, Swindon when **William HOOPER** retired.

1866:	Born January 9th 1866 at 31 Union Street, East Stonehouse, Plymouth
1894:	Marries Eleanor Florence M. Maltby.
1911 Census:	Living at Tower Studio, Sea Front on Herne Bay.
1923 Kelly's:	6 Cromwell Street, Swindon.
1926 Kelly's:	6 Cromwell Street, Swindon.
1928 S&D YB:	6 Cromwell Street ('photographer').
1936 S&D YB:	6 Cromwell Street, Swindon.
1939 Register:	The Grey Cottage, Prospect Road, Hungerford ('professional photog. retired').
1941:	Fred dies March 14th 1941 at Hungerford.

References:
COSP: 1921-1936
Pho Wilts: 6 Cromwell Street, Swindon (1923-1935).

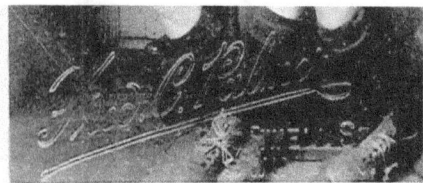 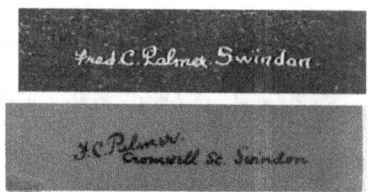

Fred. C. Palmer, The Studio, Cromwell Street, Swindon.

PALSER, Dennison Howard (1881-1917)

According to the Part 3 of the series of books by the Wroughton History Group, Dennison Palser was a keen cricketer and one of the very first photographers in Wroughton. His parents ran the Tower Stores (see also **J.W. DECENT** and **Thomas KING**), and he used part of their premises for his photography work, specializing in local sports teams and family group portraits.

1882:	Non-conformist baptism in Stonehouse, Gloucestershire.
1901 Census:	Living with his parents in Wroughton High Street.
1911 Census:	Living in Wroughton High Street ('photographer').
1917:	Dennison dies aged 36.

References:
Wroughton LHG: *Wroughton History*, Part 3, p.91 (the Palser family).

PASSMORE, Hercules (1812–1864)

Hercules Passmore was the father of **Richard Keylock PASSMORE**. The photographic business began as H. & R. Passmore. It is suspected that Hercules was included in order to give some business credibility, given Richard's young age at the time.

1812:	Hercules born in Bristol.
1851 Census:	Living at 30 Albert Street, Old Swindon ('painter').
1864:	Hercules dies in 1864 aged 52 and is buried at Christ Church, Old Swindon on November 2nd 1864.

Reference:
COSP   1862-1863

PASSMORE, Richard Keylock (1845–1927)

Richard Keylock PASSMORE was one of the very earliest Swindon photographers. His is the only photographer's advertisement in the 1864 Dore's Almanac. Richard's son Arthur Dennis Keylock Passmore (born 1871) became an eminent Swindon archaeologist and antiquarian.

1845:	Richard is born in Bristol.
1861 Census:	Victoria Street, Old Swindon ('artist in photo').
1864 Dore's:	Victoria Street, Old Swindon (with an illustrated advertisement).
1868 Voters:	Victoria Street, Old Swindon.
1869 SA&D:	Victoria Street, Swindon - listed as 'painter'.
1871 Census:	1 Victoria Street, Swindon ('painter & glazier'), living with his mother.
1872:	Marries Jane Thorp.
1881 Census:	Victoria Street ('painter – employ two men').
1891 Census:	Wood Street, Swindon ('cabinet maker & paper hanger').
1901 Census:	29 Wood Street, Swindon ('furniture dealer').

1903 Kelly's: Listed at 29 Wood Street ('antique furn. dlr.').
1911 Census: 29 Wood Street, Swindon ('antique dealer').
1920 Kelly's: 29 Wood Street, Swindon ('antique furn. dlr.').
1927:   Richard dies aged 83, and is buried at Christ Church, Swindon on January 28th 1927.

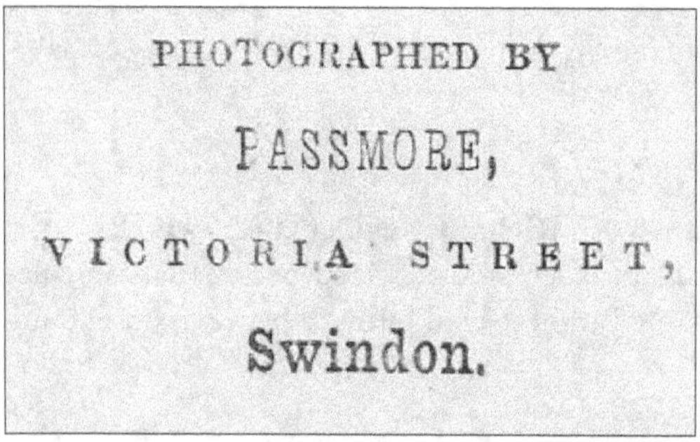

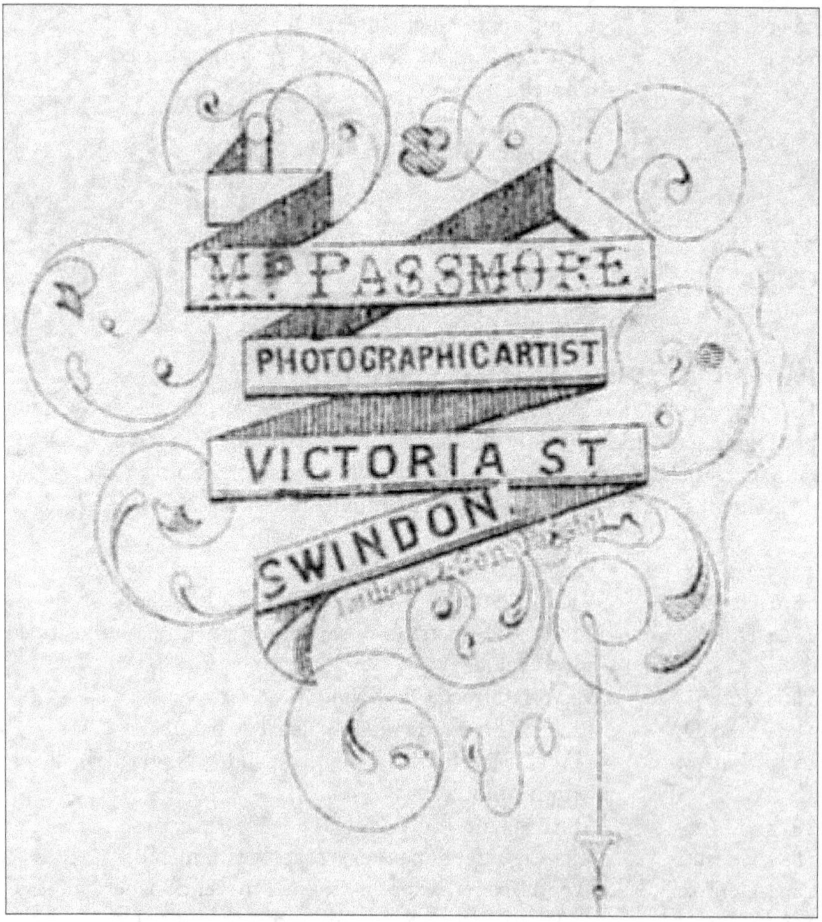

PHOTOGRAPHED BY

PASSMORE,

VICTORIA STREET,

Swindon.

R PASSMORE,
PHOTOGRAPHER,
Victoria Street,
SWINDON.

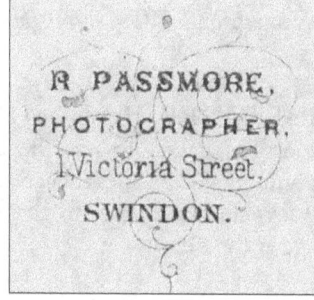

Mr PASSMORE
PHOTOGRAPHIC ARTIST
VICTORIA ST
SWINDON

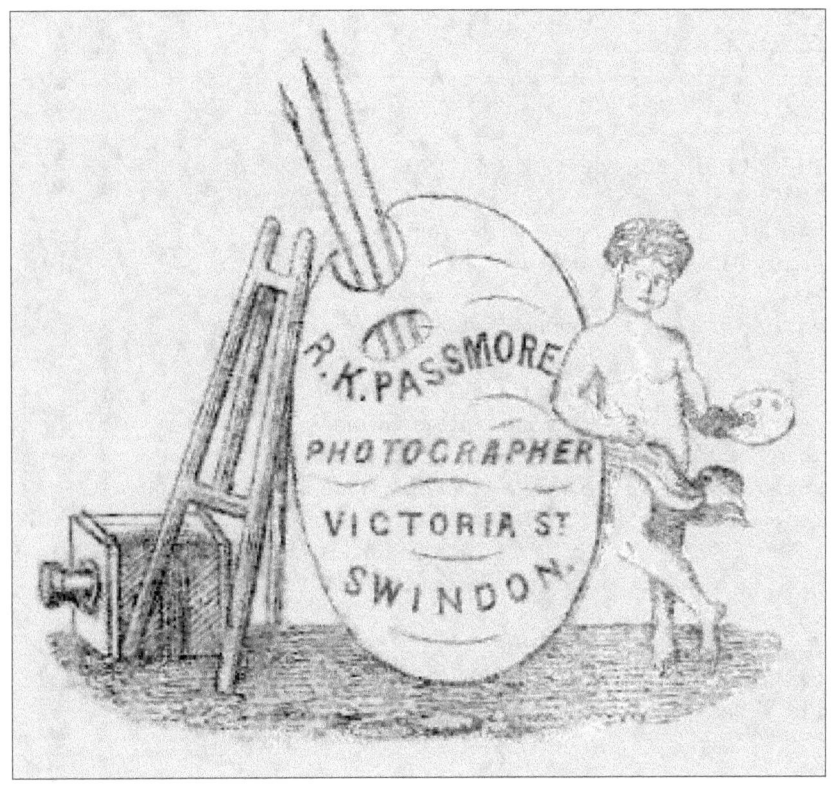

References:

Child, Mark: *The Swindon Book Companion* (entry p.87).
Pho Wilts: Victoria Street, Swindon (1864-1870).

PINNOCK, Charles Alfred (1863–1952)

Charles Pinnock was a photographer and musician, and the brother of **Henry PINNOCK**.

1863:	Born in Stratton St. Margaret.
1881 Census:	Living at Swindon Road, Pidgeon Row, Stratton St. Margaret ('GWR labourer').
1886:	Marries Mary Ann Fisher.
1891 Census:	Back Lane in Tetbury, Gloucestershire ('photographer').
1911 Census:	31 Bostock Road, Abingdon ('musician').
1920 Kelly's:	Listed as 'photographer, 171 Victoria Road'.
1928 S&D YB:	171 Victoria Road ('photographer').
1939 S&D YB:	171 Victoria Road ('photographer').
1952:	Charles dies aged 86, and is buried at Whitworth Road Cemetery, Swindon on February 2nd 1952.

C. A. Pinnock   •   *Stratton* •

PINNOCK, Charles Alfred (1904–1937)

Charles Alfred Pinnock was the son of **Henry PINNOCK**.

1904:	Charles is born in Stratton St. Margaret.
1911 Census:	Living at Coles Buildings in Stratton St. Margaret.
1923 Kelly's:	171 Victoria Road, Swindon.
1926 S&D YB:	171 Victoria Road, Swindon.
1931 Kelly's:	171 Victoria Road, Swindon.
1935 Kelly's:	171 Victoria Road, Swindon.
1937:	Charles dies aged 32, and is buried on February 10th 1938 at Stratton Green Lane Baptist Church.

References:

COSP	1920-1940
Pho Wilts:	171 Victoria Road, Swindon (1920-1935).

PINNOCK, Henry (1874–1950)

Henry Pinnock was the father of **Charles Alfred Pinnock (1904-1937)** and the brother of **Charles Alfred PINNOCK (1863-1952)**. He and his son may only have been an amateur photographers, unlike his brother.

1874:	Born at Stratton.
1903:	Marries Martha Annie Mulcock.
1911 Census:	Living at Coles Buildings, Stratton St. Margaret, Swindon ('GWR furnaceman').
1939 Register:	7 Kingsdown Road, Stratton St. Margaret ('furnaceman – retired').
1950:	Henry dies aged 76.

References:

Stratton in Camera:	Henry's photograph of the willow on Ermin Street, on page 5.

PROTHEROE and SIMONS

This was the family business of **James Smith PROTHEROE** and his nephew

Thomas Henry SIMONS, both from Swansea. They operated at 30 Regent Street and later at 15 Victoria Road, until James died in 1929, Thomas continued the business alone at this address under the name **T.H. SIMONS** until his death in 1960.

1903.Kelly's:	Listed as 'photographers' at 30 Regent Street, Swindon.
1907 Kelly's:	15 Victoria Road, Swindon.
1911 Kelly's:	15 Victoria Road, Swindon.
1915 Kelly's:	15 Victoria Road, Swindon.
1923 Kelly's:	15 Victoria Road, Swindon.
1926 S&D YB:	15 Victoria Road, Swindon.
1928 S&D YB:	15 Victoria Road, Swindon.
1929:	Death of James Smith Protheroe.
1931 Kelly's:	Listed at 15 Victoria Road, Swindon.
1960:	Death of Thomas Henry Simons.

References:

Child, Mark:	*The Swindon Book Companion (*entry pp.90-91).
COSP	c1900-1928
Pho Wilts:	30 Regent Street, Swindon (1903).
Pho Wilts:	15 Victoria Road, Swindon (1907-1931).

PROTHEROE & SIMONS,

Artists and Photographers,

15, VICTORIA RD., SWINDON.

Special Line : Our LIFE-LIKE PORTRAITS (in suitable Frames).
BEST VALUE OBTAINABLE.

Protheroe & Simons' Sepia and Sketch Portraits are unsurpassed.

Protheroe & Simons
15 VICTORIA RD
SWINDON

Published by Protheroe & Simons, Swindon. (Copyright).

Published by Protheroe & Simons, 15 Victoria Rd. Swindon.

PROTHEROE, James Smith (1858–1929)

James Smith Protheroe operated from the premises at 30 Regent Street, New

Swindon. This is an address which was previously held by **Charles CANNON**. By 1903 the business seems to have become **PROTHEROE AND SIMONS**, which James ran with his nephew **Thomas Henry SIMONS**.

c1858:	Born in Swansea, Glamorgan.
1889 Kelly's:	30 Regent Street, New Swindon.
1890 Bennett's:	30 Regent Street, Swindon.
1891 Census:	30 Regent Street, New Swindon ('photographer'). His nephew, Thomas H. SIMONS is employed as an apprentice.
1899 Kelly's:	30 Regent Street, Swindon.
1901 Census:	96 Victoria Rd, Swindon ('photog.'). This is an address later occupied by **Henry HEMMINS**.
c1904:	Marries Fanny Jane Redman.
1911 Census:	177 Victoria Road, Swindon ('assessor & collector of taxes').
1920 Kelly's:	Listed as 'Collector of income tax, 15 Victoria Road'.
1929:	James dies aged 72 on October 28th 1929, and is buried in Swindon.
1929 Probate:	December 20th 1929 (£6897 3s 4d).

References:

Child, Mark:	*The Swindon Book Companion* (entry pp.90-91).
COSP:	1884-c1900
North Wilts Herald:	November 1st 1929 (obituary).
Pho Wilts:	30 Regent Street, Swindon (1890-1898).
WAM:	Vol. 45, p. 104 (obituary).
Wiltshire Times:	March 15th 1919, p.10 (uncontested as County Councillor for East Ward in Swindon).

PROTHEROE James Smith of 150 Victoria-road Swindon Wiltshire died 27 October 1929 at Eiriaufa Newton Villas Mumbles Glamorganshire Probate London 20 December to Henry Bartlett Payne solicitor's clerk Thomas Henry Simons photographer and Douglas Charles Adey Morrison solicitor. Effects £6897 3s 4d'
1929 probate for James Smith Protheroe.

J.S. Protheroe. Died Oct. 28th. Buried at Swindon. Born at Swansea he came to Swindon in the early eighties and for some years carried on the business of a photographer in Regent Street. Thirty years ago he became tax collector for Swindon and carried out the duties until recently. He took a very prominent part in the public life of Swindon. For over 30 years he was chairman of the Swindon and Highworth Board of Guardians, and for 26 years from its foundation as a Swindon Traders' Association on a small scale in 1894, he was hon. Sec. to the Swindon Chamber of Commerce.

He was a prominent Freemason. He was the first secretary of the Swindon Branch of the National Farmers' Union, and later on secretary to the County Executive. As a justice of the Peace for the county he was regular in his attendance on the Swindon bench. He long been a member of the Wilts County Council, and from his deep interest in educational matters a member of the County Education Committee. He was chairman of the Wilts Joint Vagrancy Committee, and a member of the Wilts County Mental Hospital Management Committee, and of the Swindon Victoria Hospital Committee. He had for about 50 years conducted the choir at the Baptist Tabernacle. There was no busier man in Swindon, and few who will be more missed.

Obituary from *WAM* Vol. 45 (p.104)

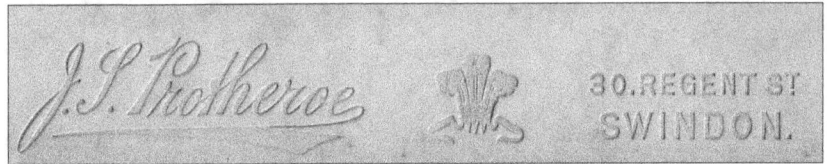

PROTHEROE, T.
References:
Pho Wilts: 30 Regent Street (1880).

PURNELL, H.
References:
COSP: 1917
Pho Wilts: 88 Cricklade Road, Swindon (1917).

QUEEN ANNE STUDIO – See George E. Stone.

REGENT PORTRAIT GALLERY
Found stamped on the back of a postcard, possible 1913-1914. The address is given as 30 Regent Street, Swindon:

*

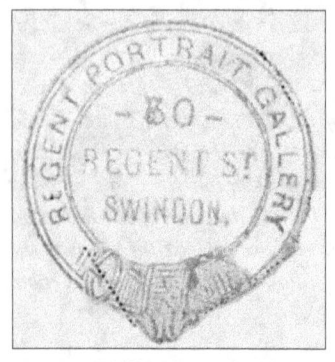 

REGENT STUDIO(S)
References:
COSP: 1911-1912

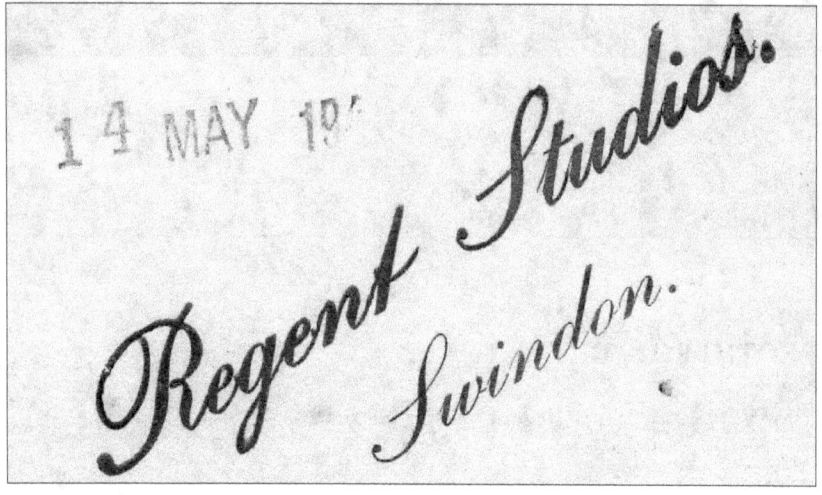

REGENT STUDIOS
1949 S&D YB: Listed at 29 Regent Street, Swindon.

References:
COSP: 1939-1950

RICHARDS, Thomas (1870–1959)
Thomas Richards was possibly only ever an amateur, He was the brother-in-law of **William HOOPER**, working in the 1890s and producing *carte de visite* from his home address at 22 Merton Street and also at 15 Medgbury Road.

1870:	Born in 1870 in Swindon.
1891 Census:	14 Medgbury Road, Swindon ('clerk builders')
1892:	Marries Alice Kate Stroud.
1901 Census:	15 Medgbury Road, Swindon ('railway clerk').
1911 Census:	10 London Street, Swindon ('railway clerk').
1939 Register:	10 London Street, Swindon ('railway clerk – retired').
1959:	Thomas dies in Swindon and buried on October 10th 1959 at Radnor Street Cemetery.

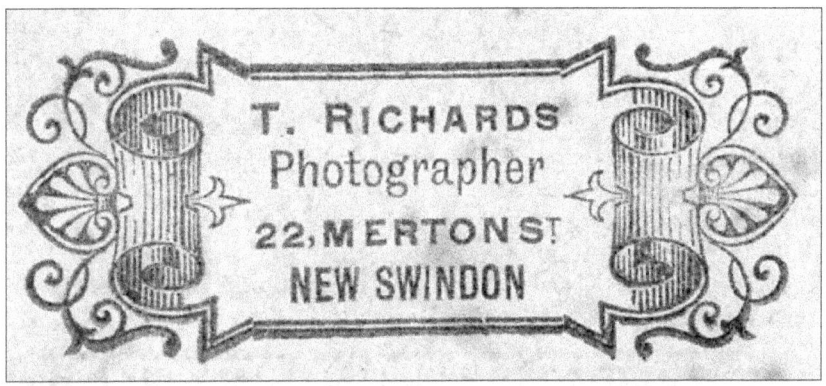

ROLLINS, William (1852–1883)

The mark of 'W. Rollins New Swindon' was found on the back of a Victorian *carte de visite*.

c1852:	Born in Datchet, Berkshire.
1871 Census:	Living at 22 Reading Street, New Swindon ('baker')
1881 Census:	Beer House, 6 Carfax Street, Swindon ('beer house keeper')
1883:	William dies April 7th 1883, aged 31, and is buried at Radnor Street Cemetery, Swindon on April 7th 1883. At the time he was living at Oxford Street, New Swindon.

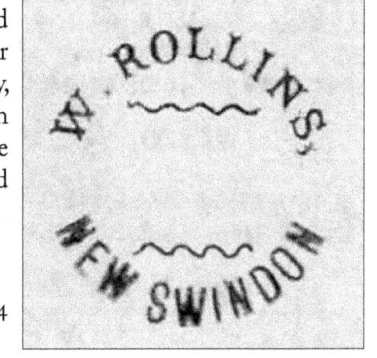

References:
Swindon Advertiser: April 14th 1883, p.4 (death notice).

ROSS, Martin

From a Swindon Police Court notice:

ANOTHER REMAND. – Martin Ross, photographer, late of Thomas-street, Rodbourne-road, Swindon, was brought up on remand charged with obtaining by false pretences a camera and other articles, the property of Silas Daniel, chemist, of Regent-street, Swindon, on October 24th.- On the application of Supt. Robinson, the case was remanded till Monday.

Swindon Advertiser, December 29th 1899, p.6.

RYDILL, Louis R.

Louis R. Rydill was an Edwardian bookseller and postcard publisher. He initially had premises at 42 Bridge Street in 1902, then at 8 Regent Street from 1903 onwards. He was also chairman of the 'Swindon Shop Assistants'.

1903 Kelly's:	Listed as 'Rydill, Louis R., Bookseller, 8 Regent Street'.
1906 Voters:	8 Regent Street, Swindon.

REVOLUTION IN POST CARDS !–Six Beautiful POSTCARDS OF SWINDON, comprising Views of Town Hall, Tram Centre, Town Gardens, G.W.R. Park, Technical Schools and Coate ; One Penny the Six ! – RYDILL's, 8, Regent Street, Swindon.

Swindon Advertiser, June 16th 1905.

BOOKS! BOOKS!! BOOKS!!!

47, BRIDGE STREET, SWINDON.

MR. L. R. RYDILL, the celebrated Book Auctioneer, will OFFER by PUBLIC AUCTION, at the above address, on DECEMBER 4th and following nights,

25,500 VOLUMES OF BOOKS,

comprising Standard Works in every department of literature, in Cloth and Leather Bindings.

Sale Every Evening at Seven o'clock.

Swindon Advertiser, November 28th 1902

References:
Swindon Advertiser: November 28th 1902, p.1.
Swindon Advertiser: June 16th 1905, p.6 (advertisement).

SANDERSON, George William (1862–1915)

For a while G.W. Sanderson operated an Old Swindon photography business at 59 Prospect, Old Swindon.

1862:	Born in Stepney, London.
1901 Census:	Tennyson Road, Bath ('living on own means').
1911 Census:	16 Tennyson Road, Bath ('photographer') with wife Ella.
1915:	George dies aged 52, and is buried at Locksbrook Cemetery, Bath.

References:
Bath Chronicle: March 20th 1915, p.2 and p.5 (obituary and death notice).

SANGSTER, A.

A very short-lived commercial photographer in Old Swindon. According to advertisements found in Swindon Advertiser throughout September and October 1865, S. Sangster was a 'landscape and portrait photographer' based at 3 Cricklade Street, Old Swindon.

References:
Swindon Advertiser: September 4th 1865, p.1 (advertisement).
Swindon Advertiser: September 18th 1865, p.1 (advertisement).
Swindon Advertiser: October 30th 1865, p.1 (advertisement).

PHOTOGRAPHY. – A. SANGSTER, LANSCAPE and PORTRAIT PHOTOGRAPHER, has commenced business at 3, Cricklade Street, where photography will be carried on in all its branches. Portraits at the lowest possible remunerative prices.
Advetisement from the Swindon Advertiser, September 4th 1865

SARGENT BROS.

A regional Edwardian photography business which ran studios in Birmingham, Bristol, Cardiff, Newport and at Wellington Street in New Swindon.

1903 Kelly's: Wellington Street, Swindon.

References:
COSP: 1901-1903
Pho Wilts: Wellington Street, Swindon (1903).

SAVILLE, William Henry (1876–1952)

1876:   Born on June 29th 1876.
1911 Census: 2 Ordnance Terrace, Chatham, Kent ('photographer').
1915 Kelly's: Listed at 343 Ferndale Road, Swindon.
1939 Register: Recorded at 49-53 Public Assistance Institution, Rowden Hill, Chippenham ('photographer's own account').
1952:   William dies aged 75.

References:
COSP: 1915
Pho Wilts: 343 Ferndale Road, Swindon (1915).

SHAWYER, Arthur John

Whilst his family was well-known as Old Town chemists, A.J. Shawyer is described in the *Western Daily Press* as 'a photographer carrying on business as A.J. Shawyer and Company at Cricklade Street, Swindon'. This is in a 1934 article which reports on an obscenity trial following A.J. Shawyer's concerns about a set of negatives he had received.

1920 Kelly's: Listed as 'Shawyer, A.J. & Co, Chemists, 12 Wood Street & 22 Faringdon Street'.
1939 S&D YB: Listed as a 'chemist and photographic agent' at 12 Wood Street and 7 Faringdon Road, Swindon.
1959:   Arthur dies in Swindon aged 73.

References:
Swindon Advertiser: November 19th 1909, p.7 (an article detailing a photographic demonstration by Mr Hoare of Kodac Ltd. at the Faringdon Street premises of J.J. Shawyer. John James Shawyer was Arthur's father).
Western Daily Press: September 21st 1934, p.7 (obscenity trial).
Link: www.swindonbottles.co.uk/shawyer.html

SHORT, William (1836–1879)

William Short was a 'photographer & naturalist' whose photographic business was also advertised as 'The London Photographic Studio'. In January 1870 a series of notices were published advertising his move from Newport Street to 5 Bath Terrace. This was subsequently followed by a move to Wood Street. After William's death in 1879, the business was bought out by the **GREAT WESTERN PHOTOGRAPHIC COMPANY.** The surviving negatives for both these firms were later acquired by **Charles CANNON.**

1836:	Born in Wootton Bassett, Wiltshire.
1859:	Marries Charlotte Sophia Farmer.
1861 Census:	50 Praed Street, Paddington, Kensington, London ('naturalist').
1868 Loyal:	Newport Street, Swindon ('photographer, bird & animal preserver').
1868 Voters:	Listed at Newport Street, Old Swindon.
1869 SA&D:	Listed as 'naturalist, Newport Street'.
1869:	Announcement in the *Swindon Advertiser* about a move from Newport Street to 5 Bath Terrace.
1871 Census:	7 Newport Street, Old Swindon ('photographer / naturalist').
1878:	Advertisements now give his address as 15 Wood Street.
1879:	William dies and is buried at Christ Church, Old Swindon on December 27th 1879.
1880:	Probate – will proved at Salisbury by John Goodwin.

FOREIGN AND ENGLISH BIRDS, ANIMALS, &c., artistically stuffed and mounted, by

W. SHORT,

ZOOLOGICAL ARTIST AND PHOTOGRAPHER.

Newport Street, Old Swindon.

**Many years in the Strand and Paddington, London ;
Exhibitor at the last Exhibition.**

The Gentry and Public are respectfully solicited to visit W. Short's Collection of Natural History. Elegant Drawing Room Ornaments of Shades of Foreign Birds on Sale.

Ladies' Plumes made up to order, and Preserved or Cleaned.

Charges strictly Moderate.

April 3rd, 1865.

NOTICE OF REMOVAL.

W. SHORT,

PHOTOGRAPHER, AND PRESERVER OF BIRDS ANIMALS, &c.

Has removed his Business from NEWPORT-STREET to more commodious Premises,

5, BATH TERRACE, SWINDON.

THE Gentry and Public are respectfully solicited to visit W. Short's Collection of Natural History. Elegant Drawing Room Ornaments of Shades of Foreign Birds on Sale.

Ladies' Plumes made up, Feathers and Furs Cleaned and Altered.

Charges strictly Moderate.

Swindon Advertiser, March 15th 1869, p.1.

References:
Child, Mark: *The Swindon Book Companion* (entry pp.115-116).
COSP: 1865-1879
Pho Wilts: Newport Street, Swindon (1866-1867).
Pho Wilts: 15 Wood Street, Swindon (1875-1877).
Swindon Advertiser: April 13th 1868, p.1 (advertisement).
Swindon Advertiser: March 15th 1869, p.1 (notice of change of premises).
Swindon Advertiser: January 10th 1870 (notice).

SHORT William. *29 January. The will of William Short late of Swindon in the County of* **Wilts.** *Photographer and Naturalist who died 27 December 1879 at Swindon was proved at* **Salisbury** *by John Godwin Hotel Keeper and Joseph Williams Carpenter and Builder both of Swindon the executors. Personal estate under £100. Resworn June 1880 under £300.*
The 1880 probate for William Short.

Notice: W.S. [William Short] has no connection whatever with any other photographer in Swindon. Please observe above address, also name on the house.
A puzzling note from the Swindon Advertiser, January 10th 1870.

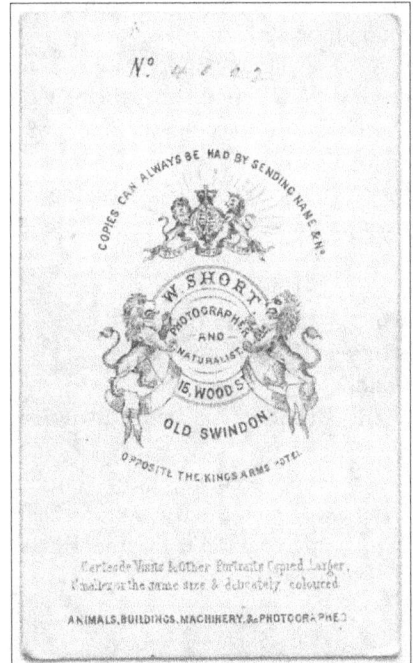 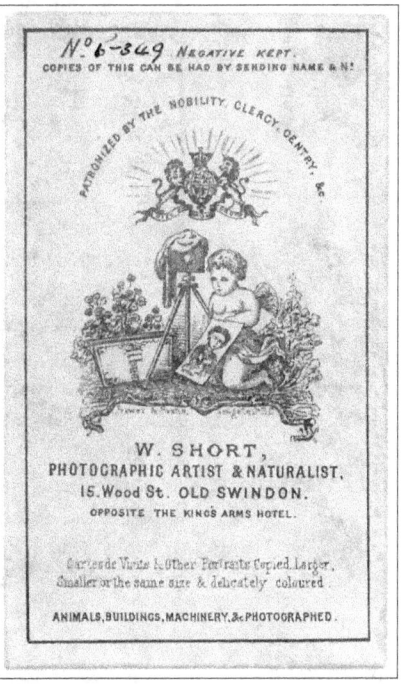

SILK, William John (1884–1954)

For a short time, William John Silk was a postcard publisher in Stratton St. Margaret.

1884:	William is born on June 21st 1884 at Shipton.
1901 Census:	Living at The Street, Stratton St. Margaret ('butcher').
1908:	Marries Selina Priscilla Hunt.
1911 Census:	Living at Westrop, Highworth ('insurance agent').
1918 Voters:	John and Selina living at Westrop, Highworth.
1939 Register:	Listed at Lechlade Road, Highworth ('provision dealer').
1954:	William dies aged 69, and is buried at Highworth Cemetery on March 17th 1954.

SIMONS, Thomas Henry (1875–1960)

T.H. Simons continued the business of **PROTHEROE AND SIMONS** after the death of his uncle **James PROTHEROE** in 1929. Thomas may have lost his sight in later life as, although he was outlived by his wife Annie, at the time of his death he was residing in the Westlecot Home for the Blind.

1875:	Born February 13th 1875 in Swansea.
1901 Census:	Living at 96 Victoria Road, Swindon ('photographer').
1903 Kelly's:	Listed as 'Simons, Thos, Hy. See Protheroe and Simons'.
1905:	Marries Annie Brown on June 28th 1908.
1911 Census:	Living at 15 Victoria Road, Swindon ('photographer').
1918:	In the final year of the Great War Thomas joins the newly-formed RAF on July 6th 1918 (service number: 265798) – he was 43.
1920 Kelly's:	Listed as 'Simons, Thos. Hy. photographer, see Protheroe and Simons'. His residential address is given as 'Ingledene' on Croft Road.
1933 S&D YB:	Listed at 15 Victoria Road, Swindon.
1935 Kelly's:	15 Victoria Road, Swindon ('Thos. Hy. Simons').
1937 Kelly's:	15 Victoria Road, Swindon ('Thos. Hy. Simons').
1939 Kelly's:	15 Victoria Road, Swindon.
1939 Register:	Living at 'Beaulieu' in Belmont Crescent, Swindon ('photographer').
1960:	Thomas dies January 5th 1960 aged 84, and is buried at Christ Church, Swindon. Probate records show that Thomas was living at Westlecot Home for the Blind, Swindon, at the time of his death.

References:

Child, Mark:	*The Swindon Book Companion* (entry pp.90-91).
COSP:	1928-1940
Pho Wilts:	Swindon Road, Wroughton (1909).
Pho Wilts:	15 Victoria Road, Swindon (1935-1939).

'SIMONS Thomas Henry of Westlecot Home for the Blind Westlecot Road Swindon Wiltshire died 5 January 1960. Probate Oxford 29 February to Annie Simons widow and Thomas Henry James Simons aircraft fitter. Effect £13591 18s 5d.' 1960 probate for T.H. Simons.

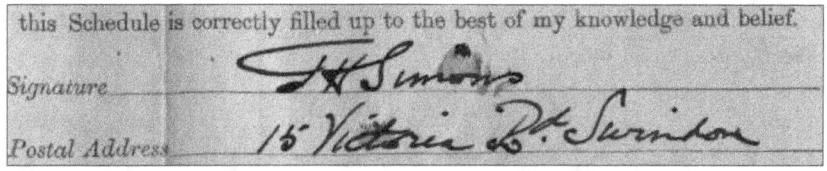

1911 Census: Signature of T.H. Simons.

SMITH, Herbert
Herbert Smith published postcards at Bishopstone Post Office.

Published by Herbert Smith, Post Office, Bishopstone.

SMITH, James John (1838–1911)
A Highworth postcard publisher with inscription often showing just 'J.J. Smith'.

1838:	Born in Highworth.
1866:	He marries Fanny White.
1871 Census:	High Street, Highworth ('printer, stationer').
1881 Census:	40 High Street, Highworth ('stationer, bookseller').
1890 Bennet's:	Listed as 'Smith, J.J., printer, High St.'.
1891 Census:	Post Office, High Street, Highworth ('Postmaster, stationer & printer').
1901 Census:	High Street, Highworth ('riveter & stationer').
1907 Kelly's:	Listed as 'Smith Jas. John, stationer & printer, High Street'.
1911 Census:	High Street, Highworth ('printer, stationer').
1911:	James dies aged 73 and is buried in Highworth Cemetery on Christmas Day 1911.

SNAPSHOT STUDIO
We suspect that this may have been the precursor to **STEVE'S**, which was later located at 9-11 Milford Street, Swindon.

1948 S&D YB:	Listed at Milford Street, Swindon.
1949 S&D YB:	Listed at Milford Street, Swindon.

SNOOK, Henry George (1848–1932)

Blunsdon's own photographer. According to Richard Radway's book '*Blunsdon – Looking Back*', Snook was also a draper who took up photography as a retirement hobby. He was known for his 'Norfolk Jacket', knickerbockers, and his tricycle. He lived with his sister Jane, and eventually they both left Blunsdon to live in Faringdon.

1848:	Born at East Knoyle, Wiltshire.
1871 Census:	South Marston ('draper & shopman')
1901 Census:	Broad Blunsdon, Blunsdon St. Andrew ('living on own means')
1911 Census:	Living at Hunts Hill, Blunsdon St. Leonard, Blunsdon St. Andrew ('retired draper')
1932:	Henry dies in Faringdon aged 85.

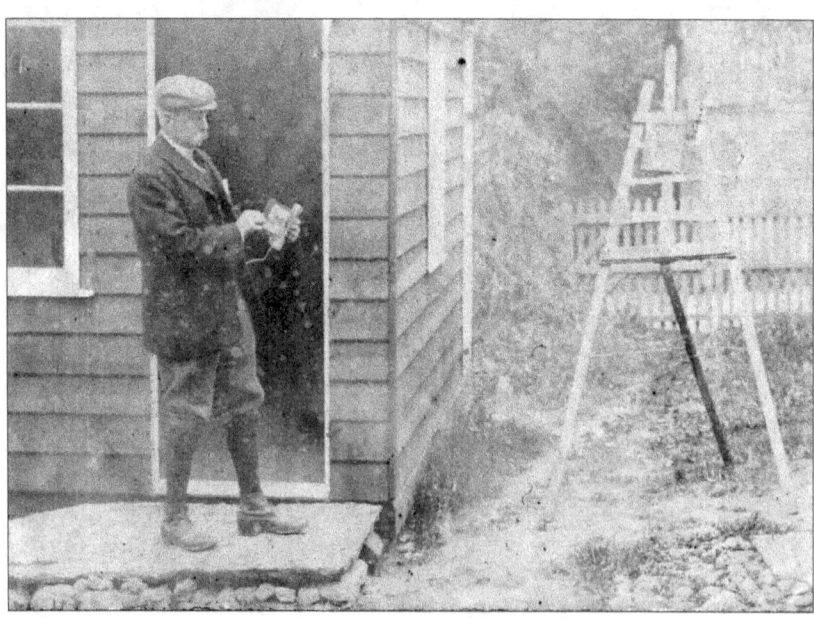

Henry George Snook outside his shed in grounds below his home, Hunts Hill House

SOUTHERN PHOTOGRAPHIC COMPANY

1907 Kelly's:	16 Regent Street, Swindon.

References:

COSP:	1907
Pho Wilts:	16 Regent Street, Swindon (1907).

SPACKMAN, Herbert [STONE & SPACKMAN] (1864–1949)

At some point Herbert joined forces with **George STONE** to promote their photographic business at 25 & 26 Faringdon Street, Swindon and Corsham High Street. In 1981 Herbert's daughter Heather Tanner published a series of extracts from Herbert's diaries: *A Corsham Boyhood: The Diary of Herbert Spackman 1877-1891.*

1864:	Herbert is born October 24th 1864 at Corsham, son of Henry and Eliza.
1894:	He marries Florence (Daisy) Ponting.
1911 Census:	Rose Cottage, Priory Street, Corsham ('photographer, violinist')
1939 Register:	69 Priory Street, Corsham ('photographer, Musician etc.')
1949:	Herbert dies aged 84.

Herbert Spackman's baptism record

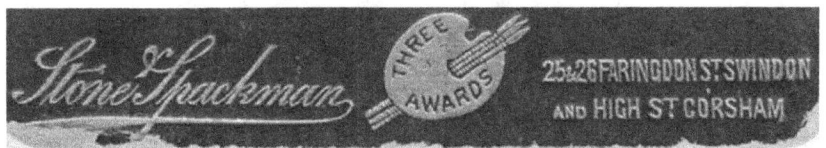

Star Photographic Company – See Henry HEMMINS

STEVENS, W.H.G. see Steve's

Steve's (Steve's Studios, Steve's Photographic & Cine Service)

A long-running local photography firm based in Milford Street, Swindon. It may have been connected to **SNAPSHOT STUDIO**. Steve's proprietor was a W.H.G. Stevens, who we believe may have lived in Cornwall and married in Swindon. He may also have been the same man whose important vintage photography collection was auctioned at Christie's, South Kensington, in 1985.

1949 S&D YB:	13 Bath Road ('Steve's Studios') and 9-11 Milford Street ('Steve's Photographic & Cine Service').

1952 S&D YB: 9-11 Milford Street, Swindon.
1953 S&D YB: 9-11 Milford Street, Swindon.
1959 Fletcher's: 9-11 Milford Street, Swindon.
1961 Swindon Dir: 9-11 Milford Street, Swindon.
1963 Fletcher's: 9-11 Milford Street & 31 Havelock Street, Swindon.
1965 Fletcher's: 9-11 Milford Street, Swindon
1967 Fletcher's: 9-11 Milford Street, Swindon
1970 Swindon Dir: 9-11 Milford Street, Swindon.

References:
The Telegraph: February 1985 (Christie's auction).
The Times: February 22nd 1985, p.18 (Christie's auction).

The sale of cameras and photographic equipment from the collection of W.H.G. Stevens at Christie's South Kensington was a sell out, totalling £35,745. A fine mahogany and brass triple lantern for special effects secured the top price at £2,400 (estimate £700-£900).
The Times, February 22nd 1985, p.18.

CAMERA COLLECTOR
£2,400 lantern
Christie's auction of the collection of cameras and photographic equipment belonging to the late W. H. G. Stevens held at South Kensington, sold out at £35,000 with a top price of £2,400 for a mahogany, iron and brass triple lantern. Dating from the 1860s. It was used to give special effects in lantern shows and was one of the first colour projectors. It was estimated at £700-900 but looked very impressive and was extremely rare.
From the Daily Telegraph, February 1985.

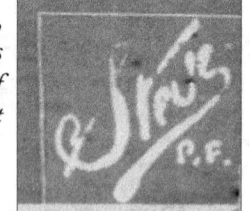

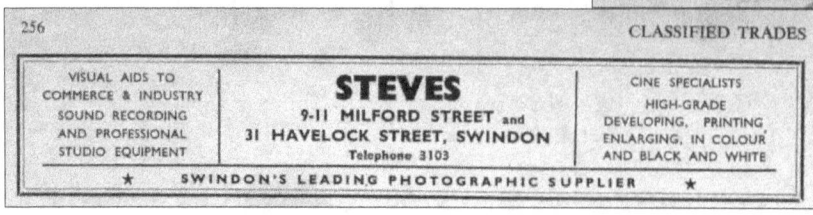

Advertisement in the 1961 Swindon Directory.

STONE, Mrs Adele Ellen (1864–1949)

The separate photography business of Adele (or Ada) Stone, wife of **George STONE** seems to have lasted for only a couple of years at the very end of the 19th Century. She then moved on to start a new business in Stroud, which ran for over forty years.

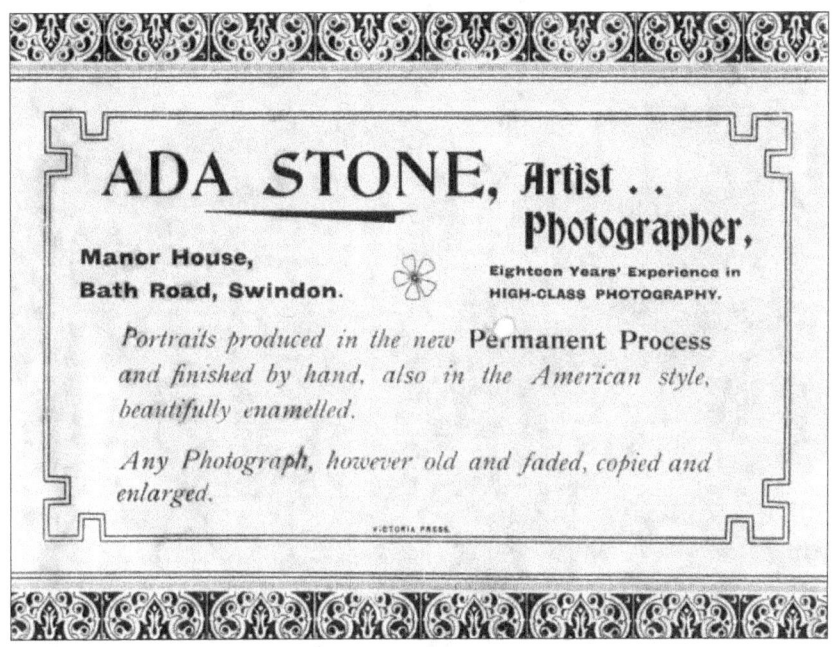

1864:	Ada Barns is born November 20th 1864 at Ashford in Kent, one of eleven children.
1888:	Marries fellow photographer George E. Stone, April 5th 1888.
1891 Census:	High Street, St John Baptist, Devizes (no occupation)
1899 Kelly's:	Listed at Bath Road, Swindon.
1901 Census:	25 Faringdon Street, Swindon ('photographic artist')
1911 Census:	Ryeford Stonehouse Gloucestershire ('photographer & artist')
1939 Register:	Carlton Bungalow, Farrs Lane, Stroud ('unpaid domestic duties').
1938:	The Stones celebrate their Golden Wedding anniversary.
1942:	Death of her husband **George STONE**.
1949:	Adele dies June 27th 1949 at Whitehill in Stroud, aged 86. She was buried June 30th 1949 with a funeral at the Old Chapel in Stroud.

References:
COSP: 1898-1899
Gloucester Citizen: June 29th 1949, p.10 (death notice and obituary).
Pho Wilts: Bath Road, Swindon (1898-1899).
Swindon Advertiser: January 6th 1899, p.4 (advertisement).

We hear that ADA STONE, photographer, of Manor House, Bath Road, Swindon,

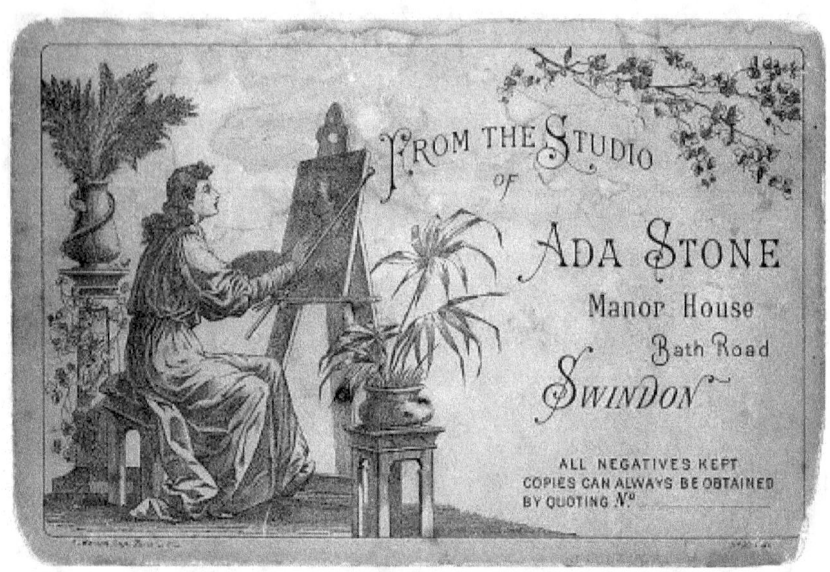

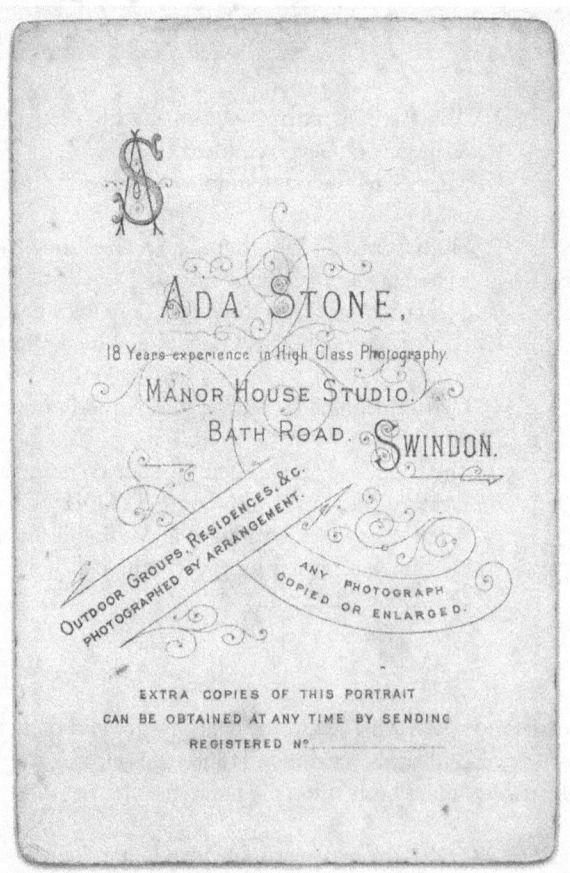

is doing splendid Cabinet Portraits at 4s 6d for 3, or 6 for 7s 6d. Her assortment of Christmas Cards, and Local Views also cannot be improved on in the town. – Advt.
Swindon Advertiser, January 6th 1899.

DEATH OF MRS. ADELE STONE OF STROUD

The death has occurred at the age of 86, of Mrs. Adele Stone, widow Mr. George E. Stone, of London-road, Stroud. Particularly noted for her child portraiture work, Mrs. Stone started a photography business in the town 45 years ago. She was joined in the business by her husband who was also a highly skilled photographer and both became well-known over a wide area.

Mrs. Stone and her husband celebrated their golden wedding in April 1938, but her husband died four years later. For the past two or three months Mrs. Stone had been in indifferent health, and at the time of her death she was living with her daughter at Beeches Green. She is survived by four daughters, 11 grandchildren and four great grandchildren. Two of her daughters live in Australia.
Obituary from the Gloucester Citizen, June 29th 1949, p.10.

STONE, George Edwin [Geo. Stone and Company] (1864–1942)

George Stone was a Swindon 'Photographer 'Royal' based at Faringdon Street (which was later renamed Faringdon Road), in New Swindon. George was initially the assistant at the firm. He was married to fellow professional photographer **Ada STONE**.

1864:	Born on April 24th 1864 at Theale, Berks.
1888:	Marries fellow photographer Ada Ellen Barns, April 5th 1888 at Ashford.
1891 Census:	High Street, St John Baptist, Devizes ('photographic artist').
1899 Kelly's:	25 Faringdon Street, New Swindon.
1901 Census:	25 Faringdon Street, Swindon ('photographic artist).
1903:	Business is taken over by **W.M. HARRISON**.
1911 Census:	Ryeford Stonehouse, Gloucestershire ('photographer & artist').
1938:	The Stones celebrate their Golden Wedding anniversary.
1939 Register:	Carlton Bungalow, Farrs Lane, Stroud ('photographer').
1942:	George dies in Stroud General Hospital from a stroke aged 78. At the time he was still residing at Farrs Lane.

References:
COSP: 1893-1903
Pho Wilts: 25 Faringdon Street (1895-1901).
George Stone & Co.:*Photographic souvenir of Swindon.*
Gloucester Citizen: May 19th 1942, p.6 (obituary).
Gloucester Journal: May 23rd 1942, p.3 (obituary).

Swindon Advertiser: December 29th 1899, p.4 (notice refuting rumours that he has disposed of his business and left Swindon. Here he describes himself as 'Photographer Royal').

Swindon Advertiser: August 7th 1903 (notice of takeover by **W.M. HARRISON**).

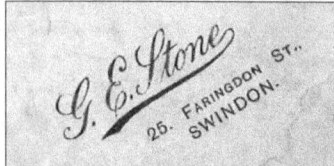
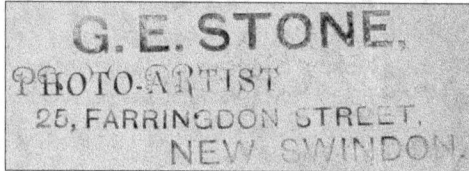

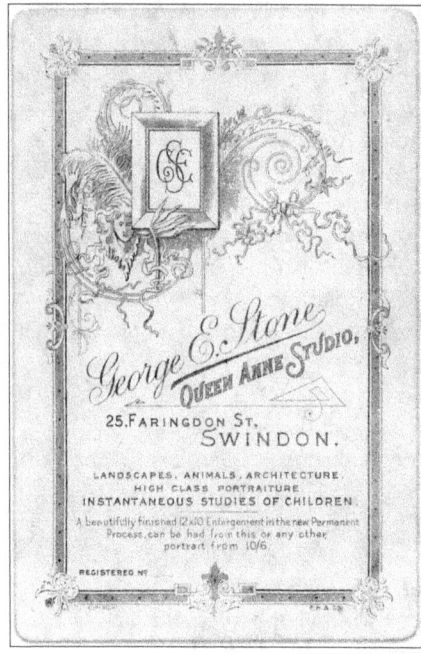
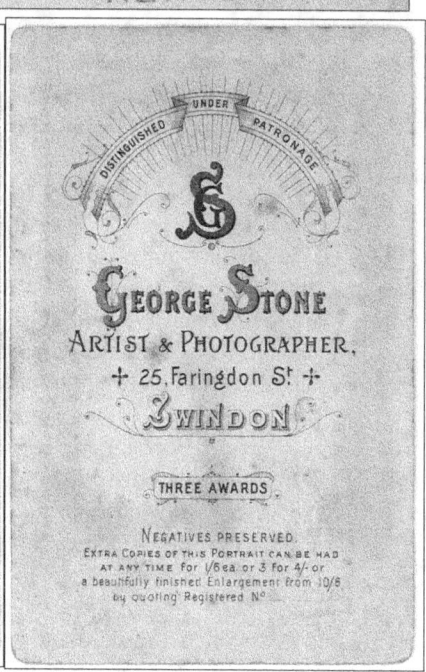

GEORGE STONE, Photographer Royal, of 25 Faringdon Street, Swindon, begs to say that the reports of Photographic Canvassers and others that he has left the town and disposed of his business is entirely without foundation. The Swindon business is still carried on by him in conjunction with a branch at Leamington Spa, and he is in personal attendance at the Swindon Studio, and all work is produced under his supervision. The best results guaranteed in all branches of photography. Specialist in the Platinotype Process, and Enlargements.–Advt.

Notice from the Swindon Advertiser, December 29th 1899, p.4.

DEATH OF MR. G.E. STONE
Well-known Stroud photographer
A well-known Stroud photographer, Mr. George Edwin Stone, of Carlton Bungalow,

Farrs-lane, Stroud, has died at Stroud General Hospital following a seizure. Mr. Stone, who was 78 years of age, was taken ill on Thursday, when he was found by his wife lying on the floor at his home in a semi-conscious condition.

Both Mr. Stone and his wife were born in Kent, Mr. Stone's native place being Ashford. As a youth he evinced a keen interest in photography, and after completing his training he started business on his own account. For many years he was thus engaged in Swindon, where he has a successful concern, and in the meantime his wife started business in London-road, Stroud, which she carried on in her own name. That was over 40 years ago, and eventually Mr. Stone sold his Swindon connection and joined forces with Mrs. Stone. Their worked earned for them a high reputation, particularly in regard to child portraiture.

Four years ago Mr. and Mrs. Stone celebrated their Golden Wedding. They were married on April 5 1888 at Ashford, and the 50th anniversary was marked with a reception at their home. About a year ago Mr. Stone's health began to fail, and although after a trying illness he was able to resume business, the condition of his heart made it necessary for him to take matters easily.

In his younger days Mr. Stone was a very acceptable bass-baritone soloist

THE
YORK PORTRAIT
TWELVE COPIES FOR
2/-
1 C.D.V. & 12 YORKS, 2/6.

GEO. STONE,
The UP-TO-DATE - - -
- - - PHOTOGRAPHER,
25, FARINGDON ST.,
SWINDON.

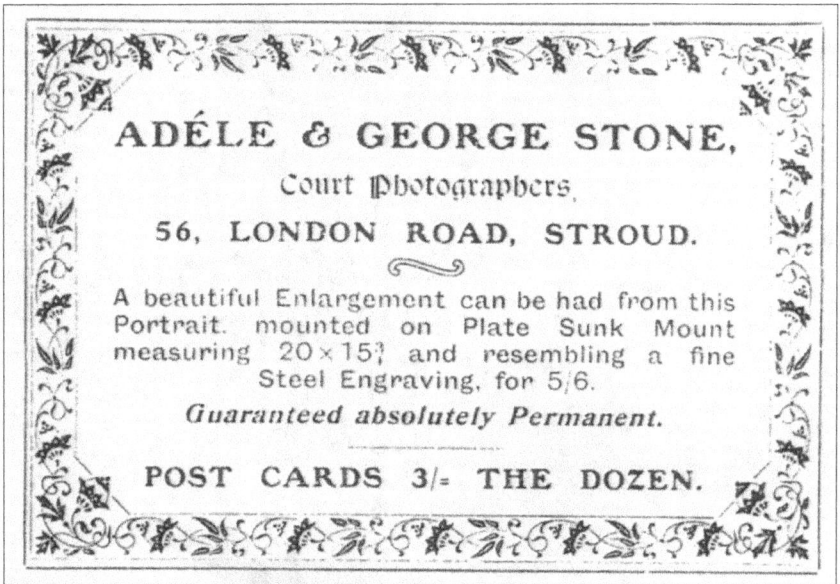

ADÉLE & GEORGE STONE,
Court Photographers,
56, LONDON ROAD, STROUD.

A beautiful Enlargement can be had from this Portrait. mounted on Plate Sunk Mount measuring 20 × 15? and resembling a fine Steel Engraving, for 5/6.
Guaranteed absolutely Permanent.

POST CARDS 3/= THE DOZEN.

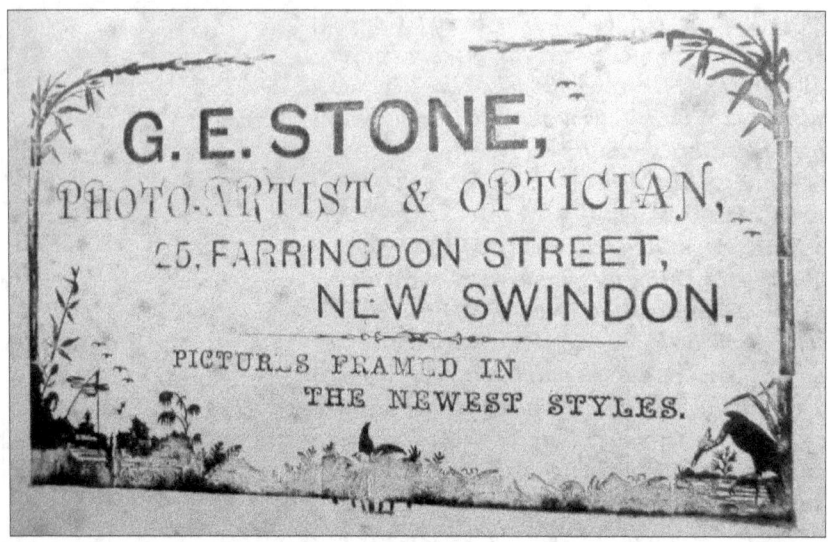

and he appeared on local platforms, often accompanied by his daughter. He was passionately fond of music, and choir and chorus singing always claimed his interest. For a long time he was a member of the Old Chapel choir. For many years he was a member of the R.A.O.B., and was a C.P. in the Pride of the Cotswold Lodge.

He is survived by his wife and four daughters- Mrs. Chew, of Cashes Green, Mrs. Caulkett, of Cheltenham, Mrs. S. Barnes and Mrs Roy Hollis, who are both living in New South Wales, Australia.
Obituary from the Gloucester Citizen, May 19th 1942, p.6

STUDIO 70
Studio 70 was a 1970s 'industrial and commercial' photography firm based at 79 Victoria Road, Swindon SN1 3BD.

1973 Swindon Dir: 134 Victoria Road, Swindon.

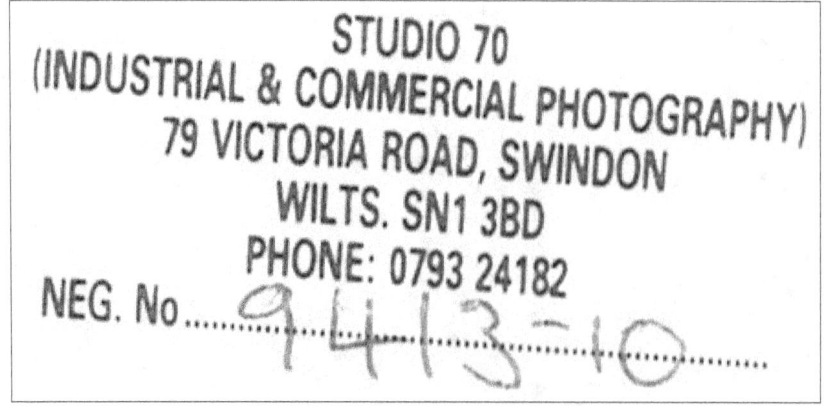

SWINDON ADVERTISER (or EVENING ADVERTISER)

Founded in 1854 by William Morris, the main local newspaper for the Swindon area did not feature photography until 1908 and the murder of Esther Swinford. It was the **Fred VINER** portrait of this young woman which became the Swindon Advertiser's first published photograph.

Reference:
Mark Child: *Swindon Book* (entry on page 247-248).

SWINDON CORPORATION

The Swindon Corporation stamp can be found on the back of images commissioned by (and copyright of) the Borough Council (Thamesdown Borough Council, Swindon Borough Council, or the Swindon Corporation).

SWINDON PRESS see SWINDON ADVERTISER

TAIT, John

A photographer based at 25 Faringdon Street. At the bottom of one cabinet card there is the imprint of 'J. Tait, 25 Faringdon Street, Swindon, Wilts', but on the back is a label affixed with details informing us that the 'photograph was taken by **Arthur BANBURY** (late **W.M. HARRISON**)' at the same address.

1903 Kelly's: 25 Faringdon Street, Swindon.

References:
COSP: 1903
Pho Wilts: 25 Faringdon Street, Swindon (1903).

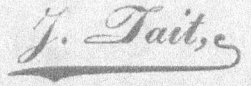

This Photograph is taken by
Arthur Banbury
(LATE W. M. HARRISON),
25, Faringdon Street, Swindon.

Found on the reverse of a John Tait cabinet card

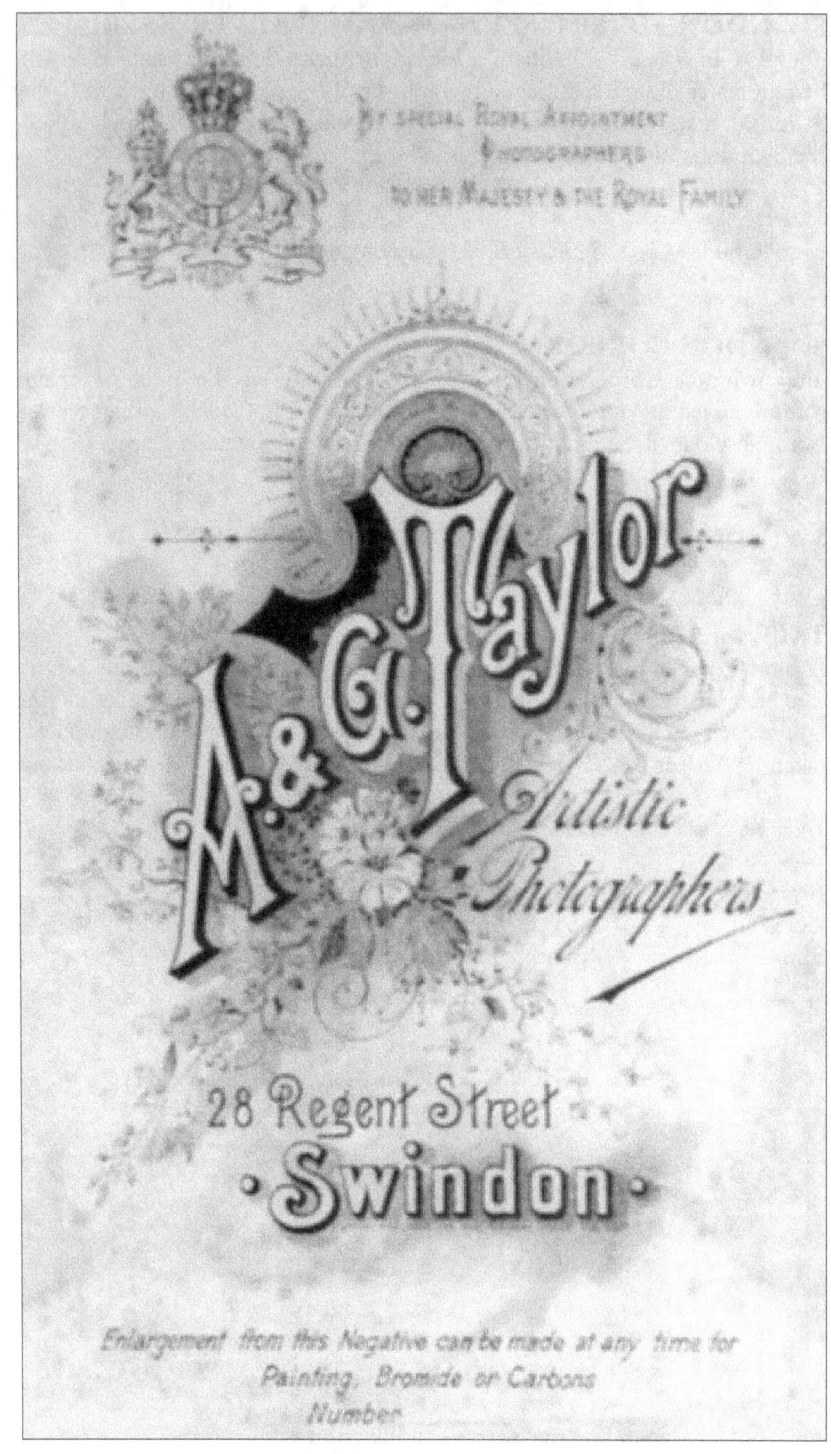

TATTON, Joseph Henry (1879–1966)

On back of a Blunsdon photograph: 'J.H. Tatton. Photographer, 99 Broad Street, Swindon also at Trowbridge & Portland'.

1879:	Joseph is born in Hednesford, Staffordshire.
1901 Census:	Living at 4 Fortuneswell, Greenhill Terrace, Portland, Weymouth ('photog's printer').
1903:	Marries Hetty Miller at St. John, Portland on April 15th 1903.
1939 Register:	60 Newport Road, Cwmcarn, Abercarn ('dentist').
1966:	Joseph dies in Wales aged 88.

TAYLOR, A. & G.

A. & G. Taylor were a short-lived firm of 'artist photographers' with premises at 28 Regent Street in New Swindon. This address was also previously the home of **James M. BUTLER** and **Zephaniah DODSON**.

References:
COSP:	1901
Pho Wilts:	28 Regent Street, Swindon (1901).

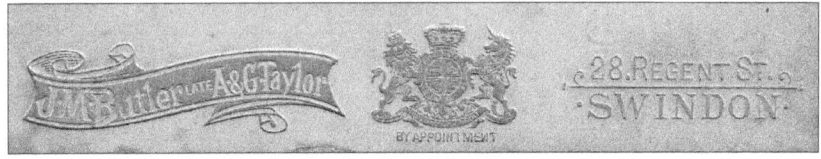

TAYLOR, F. (Frank)

1931 Kelly's:	13 Faringdon Road, Swindon.

References:
Pho Wilts:	13 Faringdon Road, Swindon (1931).

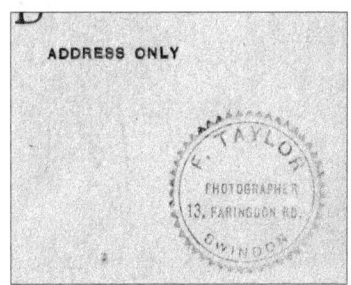

TILL, Ferrand [Ferdinand] (1862–1914)

1862:	Born at Baddesley Ensor in Warwickshire on March 18th 1862.
1889:	Marries Eugenie Harwood.
1901 Census:	124 Commercial Road Swindon ('mechanic – metal shaper').

| 1911 Census: | 124 Commercial Road Swindon ('charge machineman shaping machines'). |
| 1914: | Ferrand dies in Swindon, aged 52. |

F. TILL,   124, Commercial Road, Swindon.

TOMKINS AND BARRETT

The confectionery business of Tomkins and Barrett was a prolific local postcard publisher, in business until at least 1920. In 1905 an advertisement in the Swindon Advertiser claimed that they offered 'the largest stock of picture postcards of Swindon and District'.

1890 Bennett's:	93 Regent Street, Swindon.
1903 Kelly's:	Listed at 91 Regent Street, Swindon ('confectioners').
1907 Kelly's:	Listed at 35 & 36 Cromwell Street, Swindon and 48 & 91 Regent St, Swindon ('confectioners & hardware dealers).
1911 Kelly's:	35 & 36 Cromwell Street & 91 Regent Street, Swindon.
1920 Kelly's:	Listed at 35 & 36 Cromwell Street & 91 Regent Street, Swindon.

TOMKINS AND BARRETT

FOR PRESENTS.

Desks.   Writing Cases.

Albums.   Photo Frames.

Ladies' and Gent's Dressing Cases.

Work Boxes.   Purses.

Stationery and Account Books.

Toys, Games, &c.

FOR HIGH-CLASS CONFECTIONERY.

Fry's, Cadbury's, Rowntrees's, and all best makes in Chocolates.

Milk Chocolates, Peters, Clarnicos Toblers, &c.

The Greatest Assortment of PURE SWEETS in the County.

91, REGENT STREET, SWINDON.

WHOLESALE STORES.

Tomkins & Barrett

WHOLESALE & RETAIL

Confectioners, Stationers, Booksellers, Haberdashers,

Toy and Fancy Goods Importers.

Noted House for all kinds Notepapers, Envelopes, Writing Tablets, Ladies' Bags, Purses, Tourist and Writing Cases, View and Coat of Arms China, Picture and Reward Books, Bibles, and Presents of every description.

Ask for our Historical Legend Cards, they are interesting and instructive.

Ask for the famous White Horses (6), Avebury Stones (6), Moonrakers, Stonehenge (12), Robbers' tones (2), Wiltshire Ducking Chair (2), Devizes Castle (6), Wiltshire Bacon (burning the pig), Old Wilts Election (100 years ago), Old Maids' Church, Wanborough and Purton, Ancient Blind House (2), Maud Heath's Monument, Pickwick's House, Dickens (2), Devizes Cross, Ruth Pierce's House, Grand Avenue, Marlborough (6), Malmesbury Abbey (12), Ilbury Hill, Devil's Jump, White Horse Hill, Blowing Tone, Wayland smith's Cave, Rodborough Fort, Rose Cottage (where "John Halifax" was written), King Alfred's Statue (Wantage and Pewsey), Blanket Mills, Witney, Lacock Abbey, King Henry VIII. Barn, Wolfhall, Holey Stone, The Golden Valley, Chalford, Richard Jefferies' House (2), The Liddington Clump, Jefferies' Land, Swindon, and a large variety of others.

TOMKINS & BARRETT, Publishers the "Famous Series,"

91, Regent Street, 35 and 36, Cromwell Street, SWINDON

Viner Series
Published by Tomkins & Barrett, Swindon.

References:
Swindon Advertiser: December 15th 1905, p.6 (advertisement).

VENIMORE

In 1859 there were a series of advertisements in the Swindon Advertiser from a 'Mr Venimore Junr.' These notices claimed that he was previously the 'principal operator in the establishment of Mr Constable, Kings' Road, Brighton, photographer to H.R.H. Prince Albert'. The address is given as Bridge Street, New Swindon.

References:
Swindon Advertiser: October 24th 1859, p.1 (advertisement).

VINER, Frederick (1860–1940)

Fred Viner seems to have taken over the business of **H.R. WILLETT & Co.** at 23 Fleet Street somewhere around 1900. Viner's studio card describes his studio as a 'Mezzo Portrait Gallery'. See also **VINER AND SHILK**.

MR. VENIMORE, Junr.,

(Late Principal Operator in the Establishment of Mr. Constable, Kings' Road, Brighton, Photographer to H.R.H. Prince Albert.)

HAVING been compelled from ill-health, to relinquish his engagement, will be happy to give Private Lessons on Photography, Drawing and Painting, either in Water or Oil.

Specimens may be seen and Terms known on application at his residence,

BRIDGE STREET, NEW SWINDON.

PORTRAITS TAKEN, and Finished either Plain or Coloured.

Swindon Advertiser, October 24th 1859.

1860:	Born on January 10th 1860 in Paddington.
1882:	Marries Sarah Benson.
1886:	Working in London as a photographer, with premises at 110 Southwark Park Road.
1888:	Fred adds additional London premises at 164 Camberwell New Road
1891 Census:	Living at Southwark Park Road, Bermondsey, London ('photographer').
1901 Census:	Living at 99 Victoria Rd, Swindon ('photographer'). His daughter Ethel is recorded as an 'apprentice to photographer'.
1903 Kelly's:	23 Fleet Street, Swindon.
1907 Kelly's:	23 Fleet Street, Swindon.
1911 Kelly's:	23 Fleet Street, Swindon.
1911 Census:	Living at 30 Landemann Terrace Boulevard, Weston Super Mare ('photographer').
1939 Register:	173 Gunnersbury Lane, Brentford ('photographer – retired').
1940:	Fred dies aged 81.

References:
COSP: c1900-1913
Pho Wilts: 23 Fleet Street, Swindon (1901-1918).

ELECTRIC LIGHT STUDIO,
110, SOUTHWARK PARK RD.

FRED. VINER,
ART PHOTOGRAPHER,
Portrait & Miniature Painter.
Many Years with the
LONDON STEREOSCOPIC Co.
Also with
ALEX. BASSANO, Esq.,
OF OLD BOND STREET, W.

UNTIL JUNE 21st ONLY.

ONE CABINET for ... 1/0
ONE CABINET for ... 1/0
ONE CABINET for ... 1/0
CABINET PHOTOGRAPH 1/0
CABINET PHOTOGARPH 1/0
CABINET PHOTOGRAPH 1/0
CABINET PHOTOGRAPH 1/0

F.V. has decided to demonstrate the quality of the work he is now producing, by taking

A CABINET PHOTOGRAPH for 1/-

Children under 7 excepted. Daylight only.

UNTIL JUNE 21st ONLY.

A
CABINET PORTRAIT
For ONE SHILLING.

FRED. VINER,
164, Camberwell New Rd.
(TEN DOORS FROM VASSALL ROAD),
ALSO AT
110, Southwark Park Road.
Many years with the London Stereoscopic Company, also with Alex. Bassano, Esq., of Old Bond-street.

FRED. VINER has decided to take an highly-finished artistic Cabinet Portrait for ONE SHILLING, to demonstrate the quality of his work for six weeks only.

ONE SHILLING CABINET.

Cabinet Portrait for 1s:
AT
164,
Camberwell New Road

S. London Chronicle: June 12th 1886, p.6 (advert).
S. London Chronicle: August 4th 1888, p.5 (advert).
Swindon Advertiser: January 23rd 1903, p.4 (advertisement for an apprentice).

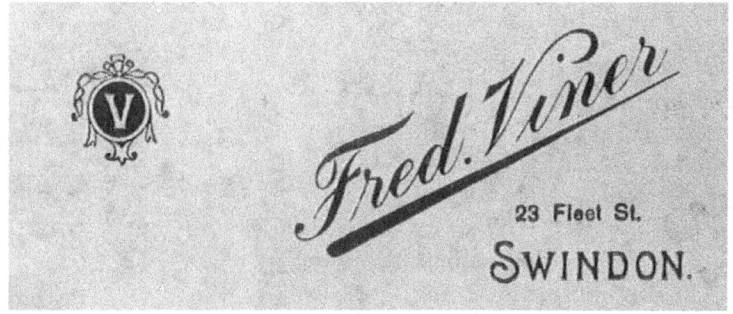

'APPRENTICE (PHOTOGRAPHY); Youth, smart, no premium, term three years; small salary commence; for Swndon Studio. - Apply, for full particulars, FRED VINER, 23, Fleet Street, Swindon'.
Notice from the Swindon Advertiser, January 23rd 1903.

VINER AND SHILK

Fred VINER and George Felix Shilk ran their 'Mezzo Portrait Gallery' at 23 Fleet Street, Swindon. Some of their photographs declare that they also operated out of Highworth. See also the above entry for **Fred VINER**. George Felix Shilk patented a 'tripod holder' July 31st 1905.

References:
Salisbury & Winchester Jnl: August 12th 1905, p.8 (tripod patent).
Western Gazette: August 18th 1905, p.5 (tripod patent).

NEW LOCAL PATENTS.

Specially compiled for the *Western Gazette* by Messrs. Hughes, Son, & Thornton, Patent Agents, 38, Chancery-lane, London, of whom all information relating to Patents, Designs, and Trade Marks may be obtained free of charge.

APPLICATIONS.

15,624.—George Felix Shilk, of Swindon, for " Tripod holder."

From the Western Gazette, August 18th 1905

WATTS, Stanley Raymond (1909–1976)

This name and the Colbourne Street address has been found on the back of some local postcards.

1909:   Born on June 13th 1909.
1911 Census: Living at Cricklade Road, Stratton St. Margaret.

1933:	Marries Agnes M. Skull.
1939 Register:	Living at 39 Colbourne Street, Swindon ('railway clerk' and 'air raid warden').
1976:	Stanley dies aged 67.

WEAR, Absalom (1859–1935)

Absalom Wear was an Edwardian 'fancy goods' dealer who published postcards from his premises at nos. 4 & 5 Regent Circus, Swindon.

1859:	Absalom is born in Bisley, Gloucestershire.
1882:	Marries Emma Gardiner.
1907 Kelly's:	Furniture and fancy goods dealer, 4 & 5 Regent Circus.
1911 Census:	4 & 5 Regent Circus, Swindon ('House furnisher').
1915 Voters:	Living at 5 Regent Circus.
1918 Voters:	Absalom and Emma living at 4 & 5 Regent Circus.
1920 Kelly's:	Listed as 'fancy goods dealer, 4 & 5 Regent Circus'.
1935:	Absalom dies aged 76.

WEIGHT, J.B.
References:

COSP:	c1905

WESSEX PHOTOGRAPHIC ASSIGNMENTS

Swindon photography firm based at 29A Commercial Road, Swindon.

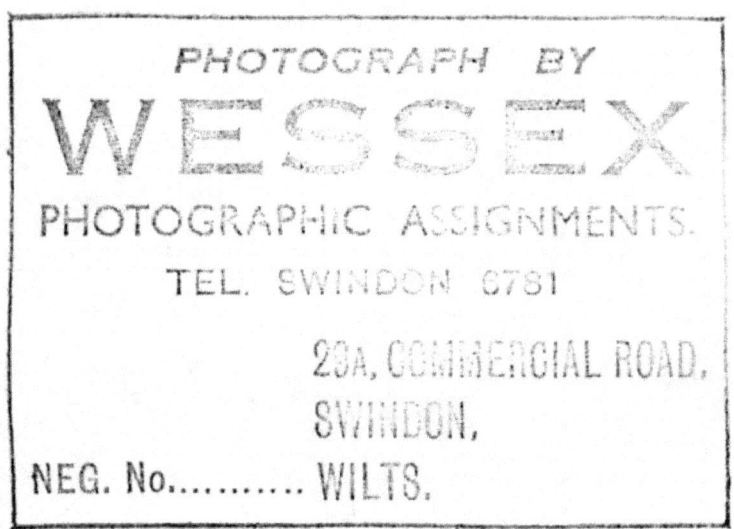

WEST, Montague Eugene

This was a firm of 'technical and commercial photographers' based at 63 Commercial Road, Swindon. He took many local school class photographs in the late 1950s and early 1960s. Formerly a prolific wedding and press photographer in Aylesbury.

1942:	Premises at 27 Market Square, Aylesbury.
1945:	Premises at 39 Cambridge Street, Aylesbury.
1952:	Living at The Old Cottages, Bishopstone Cross Roads.
1953:	Premises at 63 Commercial Road, Swindon.
1959 Fletcher's:	63 Commercial Road, Swindon.
1963 Fletcher's:	63 Commercial Road, Swindon.
1963 Swindon Dir:	63 Commercial Road, Swindon.
1964 Swindon Dir:	63 Commercial Road, Swindon.

References:

Bucks Herald:	June 19th 1942, p.1 (dissolution of partnership 'Regent Art Studios' between photographers Eugene West and Elsie Mary Garrod).
Bucks Herald:	April 4th 1952, p.3 (closure of business).
London Gazette:	June 19th 1942, p.2718 (dissolution of partnership).

AS PREVIOUSLY ANNOUNCED my photographic Business at 27 Market Square is now closed. However, all outstanding orders will be delivered from my private address:

THE OLD COTTAGES,
BISHOPSTONE CROSS ROADS,
STONE.   Telephone Stone 343.

Please address all your enquiries to this address. I regret that I shall be unable to accept any further orders and thank you for past patronage.   EUGENE WEST

Bucks Herald, April 4th 1952.

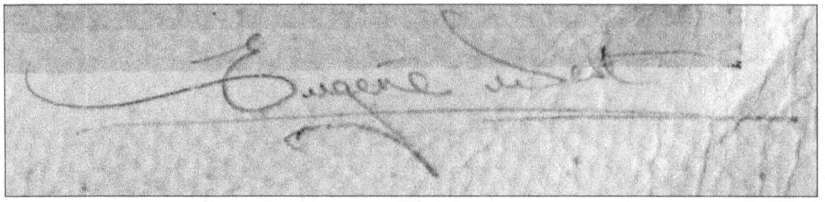

WESTON, Raymond Lionel (1895-1960)

1895:	Born in Chiseldon on September 6th 1895, and baptised October 30th 1895.
1911 Census:	Living with his family at 42 Whitehead Street, Swindon ('photographer's apprentice').
1939 Register:	Living at 57 Church Street, Clyffe Pypard? ('photographer').
1960:	Raymond dies March 4th 1960, while living at 80 Albion Street, Swindon.

WHEELER, Thomas Michael (1854–1917)

Thomas Wheeler was a former policeman who became a postcard publisher through his newsagents at 78 Victoria Road, Swindon.

1854:	Thomas is born in 1854 in Bremhill.
1880:	Marries Sarah Jane Hill on December 21st 1880 at Steeple-Aston.
1901 Census:	50 Victoria Street, Swindon ('retired policeman, now newsagent').
1907 Kelly's:	Listed as 'news agt. [agent] & confectioner at 78 Victoria Road'.
1911 Census:	78 Victoria Road, Swindon ('police pensioner & newsagent').
1915 Voters:	Living at 78 Victoria Road, Swindon.
1917:	Thomas dies in Swindon aged 62, and is buried at Radnor Street Cemetery, Swindon on April 17th 1917.

WHITAKER, Harvey Lewis (1867–1944)

Harvey Lewis Whitaker published postcards in the 1930s when he was Postmaster at Stratton St. Margaret.

1867:	Born on May 1st 1867 at Northaston, Buckinghamshire.
1892:	Marries Alice Mary Smith.
1901 Census:	Post Office, Rodbourne Cheney, Swindon ('mineral water manufacturer & grocer shopkeeper').
1911 Census:	Living at Moredon Road, Rodbourne Cheney, Swindon ('grocer shopkeeper').
1939 Register:	8 Ermin Street, Stratton St Margaret ('Sup Postmaster Retired').
1944:	Harvey dies in Swindon aged 77.

WHITEWOOD, Claire Photographic Studio

1970 Swindon Dir: Listed at '100 Cricklade Road, Swindon (1st floor)'.

WILLETT, Henry Robert (1850 - ?)

H.R. Willett also operated at Bridge Street, Bristol and Weston-Super-Mare. His Fleet Street address in Swindon later became that of **Fred VINER** circa 1900.

1850:	Henry is born in Bristol.
1871:	Marries Ann Davis on April 26th 1871 at Stapleton Holy Trinity.
1881 Census:	7 Kingston Place, Barton Regis, Gloucestershire ('photographer')
1891 Census:	Living at Hampton Road, Westbury on Trym, Barton Regis, Gloucs. ('photographer').
1898 Wright's:	Bridge Street, & 44 High Street, Bristol ('photographer').
1899:	Death of his first wife Ann.
1899 Kelly's:	23 Fleet Street, Swindon (& 5 Bristol Bridge, Bristol).
1901 Census:	Fawn Villa, Wells Road, Bristol ('photographer'). His son William H. and two daughters Blanche L. & Ellen B. are recorded as 'assisting in the business').
1904:	Henry marries his second wife to Laura Mary Price on December 26th 1904 at Holy Trinity, Stapleton.

References:

COSP:	1897-1899.
Pho Wilts:	23 Fleet Street (1898-1899).

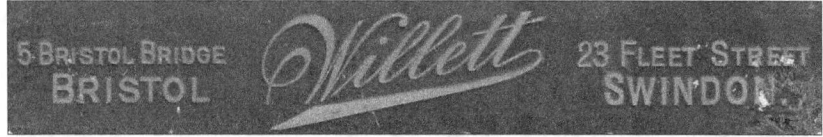

WILLIAMS, Albert see HARKEY, William

WILSON AND HUFF

A Victorian photography firm based at their Cheltenham Road Studio in Bristol but with premises at Prospect, Old Swindon and other business interests. Some of their cabinet cards are marked 'Late **Alex Betts**'.

References:
Western Daily Press: September 10th 1880, p.2 (vacancy advertisement).
Western Daily Press: May 5th 1882, p.3 (property advertisement)

'PHOTOGRAPHY. - WANTED, a YOUTH, to Print, - Apply to Wilson and Huff, Cheltenham Road Studio, Bristol'.
An advertisement from the Western Daily Press, September 10th 1880.

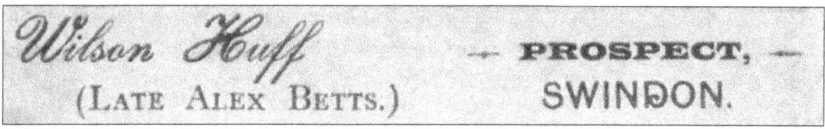

WINTLE, Richard see CALYX PHOTO SERVICES LTD.

WITHERS, C.
References:
COSP: 1917
Pho Wilts: 30 Cromwell Street, Swindon (1917).

WOODFIELD'S STUDIO see George A. WOODFIELD.

WOODFIELD, George Alfred (1864–1946)
George Alfred Woodfield was a Methodist preacher and a photographer, with premises at 13 Bath Road, Swindon. In his advertisements George Woodfield described his firm as 'Artists in children's portraiture, architectural and animal specialists'. He served his apprenticeship with the well-known London firm of Messrs Elliott & Fry. Swindon Museum & Art Gallery holds a collection of around 3000 of Woodfield's glass plate negatives and prints.

1864:	Born on June 25th 1864 in Islington.
1888:	George marries Lydia Annie Ford on December 29th 1888 at St. John the Baptist, Folkestone, Kent.
1891 Census:	Living at Hardy Street, Maidstone ('photographer').
1901 Census:	16 Copenhagen Rd, New Brompton ('photog., Wesleyan local preacher')
1911 Census:	7 Woodside Road, Kingston upon Thames ('Insurance manager')
1911 Census:	Lydia Annie living with 2 daughters at 91 Goddard Avenue, Swindon.
1915 Kelly's:	George is listed at 13 Bath Road in the Kelly's Directories through many editions: 1915, 1923, 1931, 1935, 1937, and 1939.
1920 NW Dir:	13 Bath Road, Swindon.

1926 S&D YB:	13 Bath Road.
1928 S&D YB:	13 Bath Road ('photographer').
1934 S&D YB:	13 Bath Road ('photographer').
1939 Register:	Living at 144 Croft Road, Swindon ('photographer retired').
1946:	George dies aged 82 as his home in Croft Road, Swindon.
2017:	Swindon Museum host an exhibition entitled 'Swindon in the Frame: The Woodfield Studio 1915-1939'.

References:
COSP: 1915-1939
Pho Wilts: 13 Bath Road, Swindon (1915-1939).
Western Daily Press: October 17th 1946 (death notice).

'METHODIST PREACHER AND PHOTOGRAPHER
Swindon Death of Mr G.A. Woodfield
For over 25 years in business as a photographer, and well-known as a Methodist local preacher for 53 years, Mr George Alfred Woodfield aged 82, of 144, Croft Road, Swindon, has died at his home.
A native of London, Mr Woodfield was apprenticed to Messrs Elliott & Fry, the well-known firm of photographers in London, and he afterwards came to Bath Then he came to Swindon and for over a quarter of a century he carried on his own business in Bath Road.
Mr Woodfield was known over a wide area in North Wiltshire, and also in Berkshire and Gloucestershire for his interest in the Methodist Church'.
Western Daily Press, October 17th 1946.

WOODHOUSE AND CHERRY

1952 S&D YB:	Listed under 'photographers' at 5 Albert Street, Swindon.
1953 D&D YB:	5 Albert Street, Swindon.

YOUNG, Gordon (Gordon Young Photography Ltd.)

Gordon Young was a commercial photography firm based at Victoria Road, Swindon. Its commercial work included photography for Arkell's Brewery.

1967 Fletcher's:	35 Victoria Road, Swindon (weddings & commercial photographer).
1970 Swindon Dir:	35 Victoria Road (weddings & portraits) and 29 Newport Street (commercial & industrial).

ADDRESS INDEX

The dates given below are best approximations of the years occupying the given address or premises. There are several key difficulties in creating this list:

- In many cases the photography firms may have existed at the address for longer than specified.
- Many firms occupied more than one address.
- It is not always possible to distinguish between a photographer's residential home and their business premises.
- Early records often do not include an exact address or house number.
- Many streets and roads were renamed or renumbered, for example, Faringdon Street became Faringdon Road, and Short Hedge became Devizes Road.

5	Albert Street	1952-1953:	Woodhouse & Cherry
6	Bath Buildings	1854	R.J. Artis
	Bath Road	1898-1899:	A.E. Stone
13	Bath Road	1915-1939:	G.A. Woodfield
		1949:	Steve's Studios
5	Bath Terrace		
	(Bath Road)	1863-1865:	H.J. Brooks
		1865-1866:	E. Butler
		1900-1903:	J.C. Hood
50	Beatrice Street	1950s:	A. Beaney
	Bridge Street	1859	Mr Venimore Junr.
41	Bridge Street	c1912:	Central Bazaar
51	Bridge Street	1920	J. Drew
96	Broad Street		F. Ault
98	Broad Street	1940s-1950s:	J.M. Cockell
99	Broad Street		H. Tatton
	Cambria Villas see Prospect Lane		
17	Commercial Road	1896-1899:	L. Lilley
18	Commercial Road	1893:	H. Charles
29a	Commercial Road	1960s:	D. Beard
63	Commercial Road	1959-1964:	E. West
75	Commercial Road	1901	G. Barker
124	Commercial Road	1901-1911	F. Till
14	County Road		J.S. Guggenheim
31	County Road		J.S. Guggenheim
6	Cricklade Road	1959-1961:	Eagle Photographic Services
88	Cricklade Road	1906-1910:	H.A. Beaumont

		1915:	A. Banbury
		1920-1939	L. Lumkin
90	Cricklade Road	1907-1939	G. Cox
100	Cricklade Road	1949-1952:	F.W. Hodge
		1970:	Claire Whitewood
221	Cricklade Road	1901:	C.A. Allman
250	Cricklade Road		G. Cox
	Cricklade Street	1934:	A.J. Shawyer
3	Cricklade Street	1864-1865:	J. Goold
		1865:	Sangster
6	Cromwell Street	1906-1921:	W. Hooper
		1921-1935:	F.C. Palmer
30	Cromwell Street	1917:	C. Withers
	Devizes Road/		
	Short Hedge	1859-1866:	G. King
		1862-1865:	J.S. Easter
		1865-1866:	Butler & King
		1869-1870:	King & Dodson
8	Devizes Road	1871	G. King
	Dowling Street	1973:	Hedges Wright Ltd.
	Faringdon Street		S.R. Gray
13	Faringdon Road	1931:	F. Taylor
25	Faringdon Road/		
	Street	1893-1903:	G. Stone
		1903:	J. Tait
		1903-1919:	A. Banbury
		1903-1904:	W.M. Harrison
		1923-1928:	L.C. Maylott
25/26	Faringdon Street		Stone & Spackman
48	Faringdon Street	1911-1915	S.R. Gray
31	Faringdon Road	1923-1970:	L.C. Maylott
246	Ferndale Road	1901	F.H.W. Ault
280	Ferndale Road		G.E. Edwards
338	Ferndale Road	1967-1973:	O.F. Clarke
343	Ferndale Road	1915:	W.H. Saville
23	Fleet Street	1897-1899:	H.R. Willett & Co.
		1901-1918:	Fred Viner
		1903-1920:	Arthur Banbury
33	Fleet Street		R. Lang
	Gloucester Terrace		B. Metzger
35	Havelock Street	1979	B. Bollard
	High Street, Wroughton		J.W. Decent
			T. King
			D.H. Palser
17	Kent Road		Bijou Studio

	King William Street		H.A. Beaumont
21	Lorne Street	1903:	C.H. Baker
2	Market Street	1901-1905:	W. Hooper
	Marlborough Terrace:	1883:	E. Grant
9-11	Milford Street	1952-1970:	Steve's Photographic & Cine Services
	Newport Street	1865-1868:	W. Short
		1883	Edwin Grant (Marlborough Terrace)
16a	Newport Street	1886	W. Grant
29	Newport Street	1970:	G. Young
73	Newport Street	1885	E. Grant
	North Street	c1905	E.A. Deavin
25	Oxford Terrace (The Park)	1903-1911:	J.C. Hood
	Prospect	1890s?	Wilson Huff
46	Prospect Place	1872-1880:	Z. Dodson
59	Prospect Place/Lane	1889-1898:	A.A. Betts
		1890:	Z. Dodson
		1898-1899:	J.W. Huff
		1901:	H. Dobbinson
			G.W. Sanderson
63	Prospect Place		E. Grant
28	Prospect Road	1881-1883:	Z. Dodson
	Prospect Villas		E. Grant
69	Radnor Street	c1923:	E.F. Edwards
4/5	Regent Circus	1907:	A. Wear
13	Regent Circus	1903-1911:	F. Maybury
		1935:	J. Bryant
14	Regent Circus	1891-1913:	J.S. Guggenheim
	Regent Street	1881:	W. Hart
1	Regent Street	1872-1875:	G. King
10-12	Regent Street	1951-1953:	Morse's Ltd.
13	Regent Street	1935:	J. Bryant
		1934-1937:	Empire Studios
15	Regent Street	1915:	E. Carr
19	Regent Street	1889-1890:	Z. Dodson
28	Regent Street	1898-1899:	J.M. Butler
		1882, 1895:	Z. Dodson
		1901:	A. & G. Taylor
29	Regent Street	1939-1950:	Regent Studios
30	Regent Street	1880-1882:	C. Cannon
		1889-1898:	J.S. Protheroe
		1903:	Protheroe & Simons
		1912-1928:	W.N. Ostler

		c1913/1914:	Regent Portrait Gallery
49	Regent Street	1872-1875:	C. Cannon
58	Regent Street	1885-1887:	Z. Dodson
	Short Hedge *see* Devizes Road		
15	Victoria Road		Protheroe & Simons
31	Victoria Road	1965-1973:	B. Bollard
35	Victoria Road	1967-1970:	G. Young
55	Victoria Road	1903:	W.F. Wilson
76	Victoria Road	1907:	A. Fernel
78	Victoria Road	1907:	T. Wheeler
96	Victoria Road	1899-1938:	H. Hemmins
		1901:	J.S. Protheroe
99	Victoria Road	1901:	F. Viner
130	Victoria Road	1918-1919:	H.C. Durnford
		1919-1921:	F. Colville
134	Victoria Road	1973:	Studio 70
141	Victoria Road	1907:	W.F. Wilson
	Victoria Street	1858:	Marchbank & Co.
		1864-1870:	R.K. Passmore
			Hemmins & Howell
			(Grosvenor House)
15	Victoria Street	1907-1931:	Protheroe & Simons
		1929-1940:	T.H. Simons
16	Victoria Street	1885-1903:	H. Hemmins
55	Victoria Street	1903:	W.F. Wilson
171	Victoria Street	1920-1940:	C.A. Pinnock
	Wellington Street	1901-1903:	Sargent Bros.
5	Whitworth Road	1992:	Abbey Studios
70	William Street	1915-1920s:	E.M. Cowie
15	Wood Street	1875-1877:	W. Short
		1879-1880:	Great Western Photographic Co.
22a	Wood Street	1948:	L.C. Maylott

BIBLIOGRAPHY

Bleasdale, R.H., *Album of Photographic Views of the Great Western Railway Locomotive & Carriage Works, Swindon*. London: published by the author, [circa 1881].

Bramwell-Hill, W., *Wistful Wiltshire and Other Poems* (scrapbook). 1954.

Burnett, David, *A Wiltshire Camera: 1835-1914*. Salisbury: Compton Russell, 1975.

Burnett, David, *A Wiltshire Camera: 1914-1945*. Tisbury: Compton Russell, 1976.

Child, Mark, *The Swindon Book*. Warminster: Hobnob Press, 2013.

Child, Mark, *The Swindon Book Companion*. Warminster: Hobnob Press, 2015.

Marshman, Michael, *Wiltshire: a Photographic Record 1840-1920*. Newbury: Countryside Books, 1982.

Norgate, Martin, *Photographers in Wiltshire* (Wiltshire monographs no. 5). Wiltshire County Council Library and Museum Service, 1985.

Old Town Group, *Millennium Memories: Interviews with Residents of Old Town, Swindon*. Bradford on Avon: ELSP, 2000.

Radway, Richard, *Blunsdon: Looking Back*. Swindon: published by the author, 1988.

Sheldon, Peter, *A Photographic Journey 1850-1979: Swindon in Camera*. Chippenham: Picton, 1979 (esp. pp.54-75).

Stone, George, *Photographic Souvenir of Swindon* (facsimile of a Victorian booklet). Swindon: Geo. Stone and Company, [1950s?].

Swindon Heritage, A quarterly local history periodical, 2013-2017.

Swindon Society, *Swindon: a Sixth Selection*. Stroud: Sutton, 1998 (chapter 7 - 'William Hooper: Master Photographer').

Swindon Museum, *Checklist of Swindon Photographers: 1860-1960*. Swindon: Thamesdown Borough Council, [1980s?].

Williams, Josie, *The Wiltshire Hall of Fame*. Highworth Press Ltd., 1994.

Williams, Paul A., *William Hooper's Swindon and District: a Portrait in Photographs and Old Picture Postcards* (volume 1). Seaford: S.B. Publications, 1992.

Williams, Paul A., *William Hooper's Swindon and District: a Portrait in Photographs and Old Picture Postcards* (volume 2). Seaford: S.B. Publications, 1993.

Williams, Paul A., *The Life and Times of William Hooper: 1865-1954*. Swindon: published by the author, 1999 & 2010.

Wroughton Hist Grp, *Wroughton History Part 2: Studies in the History of Wroughton Parish*. Wroughton History Group, 1984.

Wroughton Hist Grp, *Wroughton History Part 3: Wroughton Remembered*. Wroughton History Group, 1986.